INSIDE THE BLACK VAULT

INSIDE THE BLACK VAULT

The Government's UFO Secrets Revealed

John Greenewald Jr.

ROWMAN & LITTLEFIELD
Lanham • Boulder • New York • London

Published by Rowman & Littlefield
A wholly owned subsidiary of The Rowman & Littlefield Publishing Group, Inc.
4501 Forbes Boulevard, Suite 200, Lanham, Maryland 20706
www.rowman.com

6 Tinworth Street, London, SE11 5AL, United Kingdom

Library of Congress Cataloging-in-Publication Data Available

ISBN 978-1-5381-1837-5 (pbk. : alk. paper)
ISBN 978-1-5381-1838-2 (electronic)

♾™ The paper used in this publication meets the minimum requirements of American National Standard for Information Sciences—Permanence of Paper for Printed Library Materials, ANSI/NISO Z39.48-1992.

Printed in the United States of America

CONTENTS

FIGURES   vii

PREFACE   xi

1   DEBUNKING THE "ROSWELL" EXPLANATION   1

2   THE "COMPANY LINE"   9

3   THE PROJECT BLUE BOOK DILEMMA   15

4   INVESTIGATION OR EXPLANATION?   21

5   INSIDE THE DESKS OF PROJECT BLUE BOOK   27

6   THE NATIONAL SECURITY THREAT BEGINS   35

7   THE NATIONAL SECURITY THREAT DEEPENS   45

8   UFOS INVADE THE U.S. MILITARY   63

9   THE NUCLEAR CONNECTION   81

10   THE REASON FOR SECRECY   97

11   UFOS AND THE CIA   113

CONTENTS

12 UFO REGULATIONS THAT SHOULD AND
    SHOULD NOT EXIST   127

13 CANADA COMES THROUGH   141

14 THE GREATEST TRICK OF A MAGICIAN   151

15 DEBUNKING THE DEBUNKERS   155

INDEX   167

ABOUT THE AUTHOR   173

FIGURES

Figure 1.1. FBI teletype dated July 8, 1947, outlining the debris found at the Roswell crash site. 3

Figure 1.2. Official declassified U.S. Air Force photograph of the crash test dummies. 6

Figure 2.1. USAF fact sheet on UFOs. 10

Figure 2.2. Example of pages previously denied by Wright-Patterson Air Force Base (WPAFB). 14

Figure 3.1. Official Project Blue Book photographs of the burned brush and vegetation at the site of the Socorro crash. 18

Figure 4.1. Declassified cover page to the official Robertson Panel Report, formerly classified SECRET. 22

Figure 4.2. The first page of the "Bolender Memo." 25

Figure 5.1. Letterhead of one of the documents, written by Ben Z. M. Gershater, showing the tone and predetermination on UFO cases. 33

Figure 6.1. Breakdown of sightings clearly showing a surge in 1952. 37

Figure 6.2. Original photographs submitted to Project Blue Book that the witness feels were doctored. 42

Figure 7.1. U.S. Air Force press release terminating Project Blue Book. 46

Figure 7.2.   The first page out of four of the "1976 Iran Incident"
               document.   49

Figure 7.3.   The "distribution list" showing that the "1976 Iran
               Incident" document was sent to the White House.   51

Figure 7.4.   A declassified page from the Project Moon Dust files,
               as released by the Defense Intelligence Agency (DIA).   53

Figure 7.5.   This Intelligence Information Report, dated
               August 22, 1974, listed nearly thirty UFO reports.   54

Figure 7.6.   This Joint Chiefs of Staff record highlighted the
               sarcastic tone that soon invaded some UFO records.   58

Figure 7.7.   This document highlights the heavily classified
               nature of some UFO documents that remain hidden
               from the public.   60

Figure 8.1.   National Military Command Center (NMCC)
               memorandum describing the penetration of airspace by
               UFOs, referred to as "unidentified helos," over Loring
               Air Force Base, Maine, in 1975.   65

Figure 8.2.   National Military Command Center (NMCC)
               memorandum regarding the UFOs, referred to as
               "low flying aircraft/helicopter sightings," in 1975.   68

Figure 8.3.   Declassified cutaway diagram of the "Site R" location,
               as released by the Department of Defense (DOD).   74

Figure 8.4.   Declassified cutaway diagram of the "Site R" facility
               layout, as released by the Department of Defense (DOD).   75

Figure 8.5.   Memorandum, written by Lt. Col. Charles Halt,
               recounting the Rendlesham Forest UFO encounter.   76

Figure 9.1.   Example of the radar photographs taken when the
               screens were showing the UFO.   86

Figure 9.2.   A highly unlikely explanation for the Minot sighting.   87

Figure 9.3.   The official "Allegation Receipt Form," dated June 13, 2010,
               which documented the UFO encounter over Cooper Nuclear
               Station.   91

Figure 10.1.   One page from the most recent release of the Yeates
               affidavit, clearly showing much is still withheld for
               "national security" reasons.   100

Figure 10.2.   One of the pages showing the clear classification that the
                document "UFO's and the Intelligence Community
                Blind Spot to Surprise or Deceptive Data" still holds.   103

Figure 10.3.   Some of the "alien codes" used in the "Key to the
                Extraterrestrial Messages" document.   106

Figure 10.4.   Single-page COMINT report clearly showing that the
                "Top Secret" information is still withheld from the public. 109

Figure 10.5.   Letter sent to me on July 21, 2014, informing me they
                "cannot locate" all of the UFO-related documents,
                with the exception of the Yeates affidavit.   112

Figure 11.1.   This page confirms the track was at 50,000 feet
                traveling 2,000 knots, or 2,301 mph.   118

Figure 11.2.   Example of a heavily classified Central Intelligence
                Agency (CIA) UFO document.   121

Figure 11.3.   E-mails regarding the CIA's UFO tweet indicate that
                it was very much rushed and not researched.   125

Figure 12.1.   Cover page for Joint Army Navy Air Force Publication
                (JANAP) 146(E).   130

Figure 12.2.   Cover page for Department of Defense Manual
                5040.6-M-1, Decision Logic Table Instructions for
                Recording and Handling Visual Information Material.   136

Figure 12.3.   Department of Defense Manual 5040.6-M-1, Decision
                Logic Table Instructions for Recording and Handling
                Visual Information Material, held instructions on what
                to do with UFO and Other Aerial Phenomena Imagery.   137

Figure 13.1.   Air Force Instruction 10-206 proved to be one of the
                biggest discoveries I ever made.   142

Figure 13.2.   Chapter 5 of Air Force Instruction 10-206 clearly
                displayed the USAF was actively interested in and
                collecting UFO reports as late as 2008.   143

Figure 14.1.   Proof that after the Air Force received the phone call
                from the press, profiling my discovery, they changed
                chapter 5 entirely and deleted all UFO references.   153

PREFACE

It is not very often that a fifteen-year-old kid decides to take on the U.S. government, but that is exactly how my story begins. I was in high school when curiosity about the unknown first struck me. The UFO phenomenon was intriguing, it was unknown, and it sparked a fire within me that I could not explain.

Now, more than two decades later, the fascination I had as a kid has only deepened and strengthened as the years have gone on. This book is a culmination of my more than two-decade journey researching the UFO phenomenon, and my only source of evidence is the documentation that the U.S. government and military has given me directly.

Most books and websites on the topic of UFOs are largely speculative. The evidence presented in most places is controversial at best and, in many cases, unverifiable. At the age of fifteen, when I first began looking at the topic, this lack of tangible evidence drove me crazy. I wanted to change it and be different than the norm.

There are countless books and web pages about the UFO topic that you can read, and I am not trying to insinuate that they all lack a serious approach or viable pieces of evidence. But when I decided to write this book, I wanted to write it for those who wanted a serious and in-depth look into the UFO cover-up, using only official U.S. government documents as the narrative.

Although I sprinkle in my ideas and interpretations along the way, the facts in the form of declassified records are irrefutable. There are no "leaked" documents, no third-hand information, and nothing that I did not receive myself through the use of the Freedom of Information Act (FOIA). This official narrative tells an amazing tale of lies and deceit of the general public.

I have always felt since I began my research that declassified U.S. government documents are crucial pieces of evidence that pave the way to the UFO "truth"—whatever that may be.

In the past two decades, I have filed more than eight thousand FOIA requests to nearly every corner of the U.S. government and military. As a result, I have amassed more than two million pages on nearly every government secret you can think of.

This book is a commonsense approach to one of the most intriguing, fascinating, elusive, and exciting secrets that I have ever tackled: UFOs. I use only evidence that anyone can get their hands on as proof, and that is what surprises and intrigues most people who become aware of my work. Anyone in the world can obtain these same documents—you just need to ask the U.S. government for them.

There are some who would rather shrug it off. Common reactions are "It's all blacked out, and you can't learn anything" or "They lie, so why even bother?" and so on. You name it, I have heard it as people try to dismiss what you are about to read. But that is simply because they have never looked at the actual evidence nor are they comfortable accepting it as real. Once they do, their reaction changes dramatically.

Since day one, my intention has been to rise above the misinformation out there and offer something different to people just like you. My target audience has been a combination of those who have a keen interest in the phenomenon but do not know where to start, along with those that have dedicated their lives to the field and want to see the real evidence to what the U.S. government is hiding. In other words, this book is for everyone across that gamut that has ever had an interest in UFOs from the newbie novice to the obsessed professional. I will even admit I wrote this book for the hard-core skeptics and the career debunkers. I feel this information is strong enough to stand up to the best criticism that can be thrown my way.

When you see the actual evidence outlined in the next couple hundred pages—I believe strongly you will realize that there is much more to the UFO phenomenon than the U.S. government will ever want you to believe. I chose not to include some of the recent revelations about the Advanced Aviation Threat Identification Program or AATIP in this manuscript. As of the writing of this book, the AATIP story is still unfolding, and there are many questions about this "secret Pentagon UFO study" touted by the media and a somewhat newly formed "public benefit corporation" known as "To the Stars Academy of

Arts & Science." I feel without solid proof of this new project, and the true objectives of it, it would be disingenuous to speculate in this book which is based on solid documented fact; so I will save that for a future publication when more documents are released.

I hope the evidence in the next fifteen chapters will give you the starting point you need in your journey to uncover the truth. This book is *my* journey. I have invested more than twenty years and thousands upon thousands of hours into building an online database of my research, known as The Black Vault (www.theblackvault.com). I have taken the responses to every FOIA request I have filed and organized them into a massive online repository for government documents. The result is the largest privately run collection of declassified records on the Internet—anywhere in the world.

The evidence here may not ultimately give you the "smoking gun" you are looking for on your journey, but I guarantee it will give you a box of bullets when you find it.

Let me show you . . .

DEBUNKING
THE "ROSWELL"
EXPLANATION

W hen I was fifteen years old, my Freedom of Information Act (FOIA) requests were going out by the truckload. As fast as I could, I would send these requests seeking information on various topics to nearly every government agency I could find. My special focus and personal interest was the UFO phenomenon.

When I first began this journey toward the "UFO Truth"—whatever that ultimately may be—the *X-Files* TV show was in its third year on television. My late grandmother was the one who told me about it, and we began watching it on her kitchen table when I was just a young teenager.

On this show, along with quite a few other pop culture references, "the Roswell incident" was referenced quite often. "Roswell" was a household name, and although many did not research the topic firsthand, if you walked up to anyone on the streets, they know the gist of what happened.

Although versions of the event vary depending on the witness and researcher, the most popular goes like this: On or around June 14, 1947, farmer William "Mack" Brazel and his son discovered a UFO had crashed on their farm just outside of Roswell, New Mexico. On July 4, Brazel packed up his car with some of the debris that he found and, on July 7, drove it into town and delivered it to Sheriff George Wilcox.

The sheriff was just as confused as Brazel, so he contacted the military. Beginning with Colonel "Butch" Blanchard, who then passed word to General Roger Ramey, the military was perplexed as to what the debris was from and how it got on Brazel's farm.

Major Jesse Marcel was tasked to go to the farm and investigate. He collected all of the debris from the "crash site" on Brazel's ranch. On July 8, the military made a statement to the press, and the "flying saucer" story was born.

Initial reports, including the official press release by Roswell Army Air Field (RAAF) public information officer Walter Haut, stated that the military had recovered a "flying saucer." As a result, headlines flew across the nation, beginning with the *Roswell Daily Record*, who published the headline first.

Keep in mind, this was not too long after World War II had ended, a bloody ordeal that saw the fall of the Third Reich and the defeat of Imperial Japan. So for the phenomenon to begin so soon after the war, it perpetuated a hysteria and paranoia within the general public. Was the war *really* over? Did surviving factions, armed with the leftover arsenals of Nazi Germany and Imperial Japan, gear up to plan an attack when the time was right?

Alien or not, the public was becoming on edge. America had already been blindsided at Pearl Harbor by the Japanese just six years prior, so they feared another attack. They did not want to be living in the wake of the next bombing on U.S. soil. The UFO phenomenon strengthened that fear and paranoia, as sightings were being seen across the nation. From Mt. Rainier, Washington, to the heart of Washington, D.C., this phenomenon was proving it could fly wherever and whenever it wanted.

After the "Roswell" incident hit the headlines, the public went into a frenzy. Finally, their visual observances were confirmed, and whatever this phenomenon was, it was real and physical and it could crash. This seems to be the point where the true cover-up began.

After Haut's initial press release and headlines that a "flying saucer" had been recovered circulated the globe, the story was walked back by the military within days. The official line changed from capturing a downed "flying saucer" to that it was nothing more than just a weather balloon.

On July 8, 1947, the Federal Bureau of Investigation (FBI) was apprised of the "Roswell" situation. In this memorandum, it was said that the debris resembled that of a balloon. However, Wright Field (present-day Wright Patterson Air Force Base), during the course of a phone call, did not buy that explanation. The teletype in all capitals read as follows:

FLYING DISC, INFORMATION CONCERNING [redacted] HEADQUAR-TERS. EIGHTH AIR FORCE TELEPHONICALLY ADVISED THIS OF-FICE THAT AN OBJECT PURPORTING TO BE A FLYING DISC WAS RE COVERED [sic] NEAR ROSWELL, NEW MEXICO, THIS DATE. THE DISC IS HEXAGONAL IN SHAPE AND WAS SUSPENDED FROM A

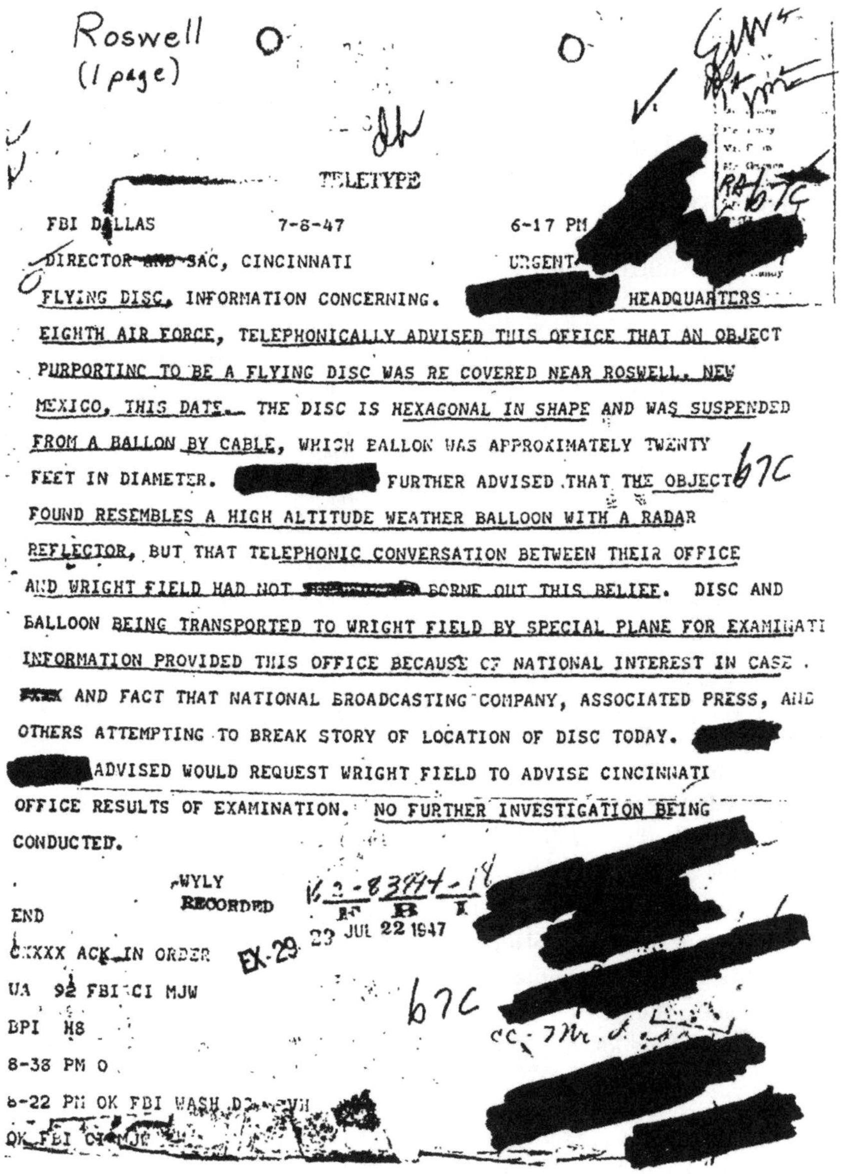

Roswell
(1 page)

FBI DALLAS   7-8-47   6-17 PM

DIRECTOR AND SAC, CINCINNATI   URGENT

FLYING DISC, INFORMATION CONCERNING.   HEADQUARTERS

EIGHTH AIR FORCE, TELEPHONICALLY ADVISED THIS OFFICE THAT AN OBJECT

PURPORTING TO BE A FLYING DISC WAS RE COVERED NEAR ROSWELL, NEW

MEXICO, THIS DATE. THE DISC IS HEXAGONAL IN SHAPE AND WAS SUSPENDED

FROM A BALLON BY CABLE, WHICH BALLON WAS APPROXIMATELY TWENTY

FEET IN DIAMETER.   FURTHER ADVISED THAT THE OBJECT

FOUND RESEMBLES A HIGH ALTITUDE WEATHER BALLOON WITH A RADAR

REFLECTOR, BUT THAT TELEPHONIC CONVERSATION BETWEEN THEIR OFFICE

AND WRIGHT FIELD HAD NOT   BORNE OUT THIS BELIEF. DISC AND

BALLOON BEING TRANSPORTED TO WRIGHT FIELD BY SPECIAL PLANE FOR EXAMINATI

INFORMATION PROVIDED THIS OFFICE BECAUSE OF NATIONAL INTEREST IN CASE .

AND FACT THAT NATIONAL BROADCASTING COMPANY, ASSOCIATED PRESS, AND

OTHERS ATTEMPTING TO BREAK STORY OF LOCATION OF DISC TODAY.

ADVISED WOULD REQUEST WRIGHT FIELD TO ADVISE CINCINNATI

OFFICE RESULTS OF EXAMINATION. NO FURTHER INVESTIGATION BEING

CONDUCTED.

WYLY
RECORDED

END

CXXXX ACK IN ORDER

UA 92 FBI CI MJW

BPI HS

8-38 PM O

6-22 PM OK FBI WASH DC

OK FBI CI

Figure 1.1.   FBI teletype dated July 8, 1947, outlining the debris found at the Roswell crash site.

BALLON [sic] BY CABLE, WHICH BALLOON WAS APPROXIMATELY TWENTY FEET IN DIAMETER. [redacted] FURTHER ADVISED THAT THE OBJECT FOUND RESEMBLES A HIGH ALTITUDE WEATHER BALLOON WITH A RADAR REFLECTOR BUT THAT TELEPHONIC CONVERSATION BETWEEN THEIR OFFICE AND WRIGHT FIELD HAD NOT [crossed-out unreadable text] BORNE OUT THIS BELIEF. DISC AND BALLOON BEING TRANSPORTED TO WRIGHT FIELD BY SPECIAL PLANE FOR EXAMINATION. INFORMATION PROVIDED THIS BECAUSE OF NATIONAL INTEREST IN CASE XXXX AND FACT THAT NATIONAL BROADCASTING COMPANY, ASSOCIATED PRESS, AND OTHERS ATTEMPTING TO BREAK STORY OF LOCATION OF DISC TODAY. [redacted] ADVISED WOULD REQUEST WRIGHT FIELD TO ADVISE CINCINNATI OFFICE RESULTS OF EXAMINATION. NO FURTHER INVESTIGATION BEING CONDUCTED.

Although the cover-up story was under way, it is evident that Wright Field was not buying the weather balloon explanation and wanted to see the material. As a result, the debris was flown to Wright Field for investigation. It would seem plausible, if the Roswell debris was nothing more than a balloon, that the military could have identified it immediately based on the composition of what was recovered. It should not have required such an extensive analysis at Wright Field. To the contrary, they were as confused as anyone in those initial days, and they felt the need for a more in-depth investigation aimed to identify the debris.

Yet despite their confusion over where the debris came from, the cover-up commenced. The military continued to denounce the "alien" and "flying saucer" headlines and rather published their own weather balloon story.

Since the events surrounding the Roswell incident have unfolded, the U.S. government and military have offered multiple explanations over the past seven decades, in an attempt to explain the legend of what really happened at Roswell. The first real investigation into the Roswell incident was published by the General Accounting Office (GAO) in 1994. One of the biggest claims in this report, which is often overlooked by the general public, is the following statement:

In our search for records concerning the Roswell crash, we learned that some government records covering RAAF activities had been destroyed and others had not. For example, RAAF administrative records (from Mar. 1945 through Dec. 1949) and RAAF outgoing messages (from Oct. 1946 through Dec. 1949) were destroyed. The document disposition form does not indicate what organization or person destroyed the records and when or under what authority the records were destroyed.

Despite the GAO concluding the "alien" explanation held no validity, they did discover that a large number of documents relating to the time frame of the Roswell incident were destroyed. Since these records were destroyed, is it possible to truly give a determination on what really happened? How do we know what really was destroyed and what those records could have proven or disproven? It appeared that this investigation was crippled from the start, but that did not stop the GAO from trying to say that it was not aliens.

The explanations continued long after this GAO report. The U.S. Air Force published *The Roswell Report: Fact Versus Fiction in the New Mexico Desert* in 1995, along with *The Roswell Report: Case Closed* in 1997. The latter has been the last, and supposedly final, explanation for the Roswell incident.

I often believe, and this is evident with these reports, if you drown the public in information, they will simply give up trying to get answers. There is just too much to sift through. These reports are not three-page summaries but rather consist collectively of more than one thousand pages of documents, testimonials, and conclusions. If we know the end result and the U.S. government seemingly destroyed evidence but is still willing to put out a "weather balloon/not alien" explanation, why read through the more than one thousand pages of reports? I think that is what they want. Take their word for it—and don't ask questions. Because when you do, you realize their explanation does not make sense.

In 1997, when the Air Force published *The Roswell Report: Case Closed*, it consisted of 232 pages. It was published within about a year of when I started doing my research, so I was intrigued by what it might contain. I took a look at the report's summary and conclusions to see what the military was going to say this time, and I was astonished at how easy it was to debunk the official explanation, even this newest rendition of it.

The Roswell Report: Case Closed offered the following bullet points:

- "Aliens" observed in the New Mexico desert were actually anthropomorphic test dummies that were carried aloft by U.S. Air Force high-altitude balloons for scientific research.
- The "unusual" military activities in the New Mexico desert were high-altitude research balloon launch and recovery operations. Reports of military units that always seemed to arrive shortly after the crash of a flying saucer to retrieve the saucer and "crew" were actually accurate descriptions of Air Force personnel engaged in anthropomorphic dummy recovery operations.

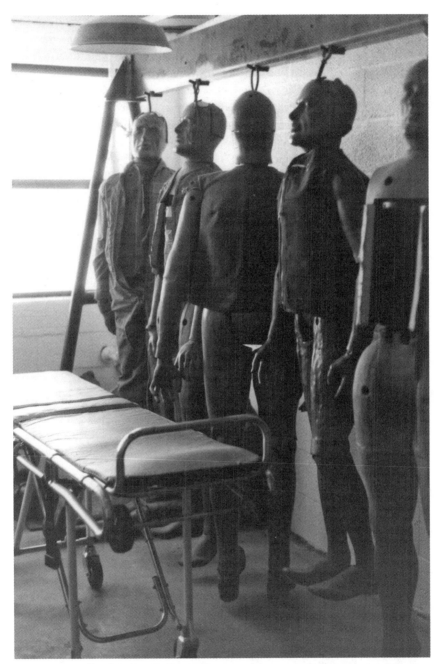

Figure 1.2. Official declassified U.S. Air Force photograph of the crash test dummies.

These first two conclusions seem plausible, right? Despite amazing researchers like Mr. Stanton Friedman, who had uncovered multiple witnesses that would testify about seeing alien bodies, the military wanted to assure the general public that they had another explanation in mind: crash test dummies.

These crash test dummies were part of Operation High Dive, a secret project carried out by the U.S. Air Force, which tested parachutes dropped from high altitudes. According to the Air Force, it was these dummies that could partially explain the multiple witnesses and their descriptions of "alien bodies" being seen at Roswell Army Air Field. Just do not bother with the facts, if you feel this explanation is worth believing.

The very first crash test dummy invented was "Sierra Sam" created by Alderson Research Labs (ARL) and Sierra Engineering Company. The year of creation: 1949. It may take you a moment to realize, but there is a huge error here in history. Roswell occurred in 1947, approximately two years before the first crash test dummy was ever invented.

Unless we just discovered time-traveling crash test dummies, how could the Air Force pass off such a theory to explain the alien bodies? The lie goes deeper and gets much worse. The explanations continued in *The Roswell Report: Case Closed*:

- Claims of "alien bodies" at the Roswell Army Air Field hospital were most likely a combination of two separate incidents:
  - ... a 1956 KC-97 aircraft accident in which 11 Air Force members lost their lives; and
  - ... a 1959 manned balloon mishap in which two Air Force pilots were injured.

You can probably more easily see the blaring error with this one. Instead of a two-year time travel between the crash test dummies being invented and the year the Roswell incident actually happened, now the Air Force is passing off two separate incidents to further explain the claims of "alien bodies." Respectively, these incidents occurred nine and twelve years after the Roswell incident, and somehow, the military feels this is all OK to try and pass off to the public. I mean, we shouldn't let facts get in the way of a good story.

What about the witnesses claiming to have seen alien bodies and not Air Force pilots or crash test dummies? They were wrong . . . each and every one of them. The *New York Times* summarized the Air Force's response to this discrepancy in their June 25, 1997, front-page article titled, "Air Force Details a New Theory in U.F.O. Case—A Suggestion That Dead 'Aliens' Were Test Dummies":

> Critics of the new report bridle at its main thesis: that civilians are confusing military activities that took place over more than a decade and falsely recalling them as a single incident. Such memory failures, critics say, are highly unlikely. But the Air Force says the witnesses are often recalling events more than four decades old and could have easily mixed up the dates.

After reading these "conclusions" by the U.S. government and military to one of the biggest and most well-known UFO cases ever, I was convinced they did not do an adequate job to explain it. In order to buy the military's theory, you needed to accept that a lot of the information had been destroyed, and you had to be OK with time-traveling test dummies and dead Air Force pilots who could bend time. All of that was supposed to account for the witnesses coming forward talking about alien bodies at the Roswell Army Air Field in 1947.

As you can see, the explanation that is given for the "Roswell incident" is laughable at best. Whether the debris was the by-product of a crashed alien saucer or there is another top secret, yet-to-be-revealed project, anyone can see the absolute ridiculous nature of what the government is trying to currently pass off as the real story.

There have been amazing books and documentaries on Roswell, and it truly does deserve more than a single chapter to adequately explain that full story. But for my journey and purpose here, I am going to move on. As a starting point, I feel that this official narrative that the U.S. government and military wants you to believe about Roswell is nothing close to reality, and the proof is there if you look for it. As to what *really* happened, we will probably never know, but I wanted to at least show how easy it was to debunk the official narrative.

I pushed forward to see what else there was to find within the archives of the U.S. government and the military, and to my surprise, debunking the official Roswell explanation was only the tip of the iceberg on proving one of the biggest cover-ups of all time.

THE "COMPANY LINE"

It was easy to disprove the recent explanations that the U.S. military wanted to put forth on the Roswell incident, but I knew deep down that was not all there was to discover. In addition to attempting to explain the Roswell incident, the U.S. government had another tale they were trying to spin to squash any public interest into the UFO phenomenon.

The U.S. government attempted to prove to me while I was a teenager that they had already investigated UFOs and found absolutely nothing to support that the phenomenon was real, alien, or a threat to any of us. On the contrary, they tried to claim that nearly everything they did investigate during their study known as "Project Blue Book," which spanned more than twelve thousand cases over the course of twenty-one years, was easily explainable.

At least, that is what their "fact sheet" tried to tell me. My original UFO-related FOIA requests would get this document as an attachment to my response letters, and initially, that was all I would get. This "fact sheet" described "Project Blue Book," which was the most popular name out of a trifecta of projects aimed to tackle the UFO topic by the U.S. military.

It began with Project Sign in 1947, followed by Project Grudge in February of 1949, and then the effort became known as Project Blue Book in 1952. This lasted until the end of 1969 and was ultimately closed in January of 1970, simply because they felt they solved the mystery.

Since this "fact sheet" has been given to me more than any other document since I began researching, I feel I should let this record speak for itself. It states, in part:

From 1947 to 1969, the Air Force investigated Unidentified Flying Objects under Project Blue Book. The project, headquartered at Wright-Patterson Air

Fact Sheet
United States Air Force
Secretary of the Air Force, Office of Public Affairs, Washington, D.C. 20330

INFORMATION ON UFOs

Thank you for your request for information on the Air Force's investigation of unidentified flying objects, or UFO's.

The Air Force investigation of UFO's began in 1948 and was known as Project Sign. Later the name was changed to Project Grudge, and in 1953, it became Project Blue Book. Between 1948 and 1969 we investigated 12,618 reported sightings.

Of these sightings, 11,917 were found to have been caused by material objects (such as balloons, satellites, and aircraft), immaterial objects (such as lightning, reflections, and other natural phenomena), astronomical objects (such as stars, planets, the sun, and the moon), weather conditions, and hoaxes. As indicated, only 701 reported sightings remain unexplained.

On December 17, 1969, the Secretary of the Air Force announced the termination of Project Blue Book. The decision to discontinue UFO investigations was based on an evaluation of a report prepared by the University of Colorado entitled, "Scientific Study of Unidentified Flying Objects;" a review of the University of Colorado's report by the National Academy of Sciences; past UFO studies; and the Air Force's two decades of experience investigating UFO reports.

As a result of these investigations, studies, and experience, the conclusions of Project Blue Book were: (1) no UFO reported, investigated, and evaluated by the Air Force has ever given any indication of threat to our national security; (2) there has been no evidence submitted to or discovered by the Air Force that sightings categorized as "unidentified" represent technological developments or principles beyond the range of present day scientific knowledge; and (3) there has been no evidence indicating that sightings categorized as "unidentified" are extraterrestrial vehicles.

With the termination of Project Blue Book, the Air Force regulation establishing and controlling the program for investigating and analyzing UFOs was rescinded. All documentation regarding the former Blue Book investigation was permanently transferred to the Modern Military Branch, National Archives and Record Service, 8th and Pennsylvania Avenue, Washington DC 20408, and is available for public review and analysis.

Figure 2.1.   USAF fact sheet on UFOs.

Force Base, Ohio, was terminated Dec. 17, 1969. Of a total of 12,618 sightings reported to Project Blue Book, 701 remained "unidentified."

The decision to discontinue UFO investigations was based on an evaluation of a report prepared by the University of Colorado titled, "Scientific Study of Unidentified Flying Objects"; a review of the University of Colorado's report by the National Academy of Sciences; and previous UFO studies and Air Force experience investigating UFO reports during the 1940s, '50s and '60s.

As a result of these investigations, studies, and experience gained from investigating UFO reports since 1948, the conclusions of Project Blue Book were: (1) no UFO reported, investigated, and evaluated by the Air Force was ever an indication of threat to our national security; (2) there was no evidence submitted to or discovered by the Air Force that sightings categorized as "unidentified" represented technological developments or principles beyond the range of modern scientific knowledge; and (3) there was no evidence indicating that sightings categorized as "unidentified" were extraterrestrial vehicles.

With the termination of Project Blue Book, the Air Force regulation establishing and controlling the program for investigating and analyzing UFOs was rescinded. Documentation regarding the former Blue Book investigation was permanently transferred to the Modern Military Branch, National Archives and Records Service, Eighth Street and Pennsylvania Avenue, N.W., Washington, D.C. 20408, and is available for public review and analysis.

Since the termination of Project Blue Book, nothing has occurred that would support a resumption of UFO investigations by the Air Force. Given the current environment of steadily decreasing defense budgets, it is unlikely the Air Force would become involved in such a costly project in the foreseeable future.

To this day, this "fact sheet" serves as the official explanation by the U.S. government to address the UFO phenomenon. I call it their "company line" as this is the standard summary of the Project Blue Book investigations, and it serves to outline their belief that they found nothing out of the ordinary.

One of the first few FOIA requests I ever filed was to the headquarters of the U.S. Air Force seeking documents on UFOs. The response I received to this request back in 1996 is where I first learned about the Project Blue Book "fact sheet" and their "official" explanation for the phenomenon. On the surface, it all seemed believable. They investigated and they solved the mystery.

If the U.S. government got what it wanted, you would buy this hook, line, and sinker and just go away. This is what I would bet money they wanted me to do, and to be honest, I bet most people give up after they receive these initial responses. They just wrongfully assume there really is not much to find in relation to documentation, except for rather dull Project Blue Book investigation files where the military claims they solved the mystery.

As I mentioned earlier in this book, that general assumption by the public is what the government wants. Do not ask questions; do not question the narrative. Just believe it—and go away. Yet there is a huge problem with this so-called "fact sheet" and their "company line" explanation—and that is that there are very few "facts" on it.

I found out the hard way that this "fact sheet" would become the top of a growing list of easily provable lies the U.S. government would try to dish out. For example, Project Blue Book had its home at Wright-Patterson Air Force Base (WPAFB) in Ohio. According to this "fact sheet," all UFO-related reports within Project Blue Book were transferred from there to the National Archives and Records Administration (NARA). They go on to state that no other Air

Force installation would have anything on Project Blue Book or UFOs. Instead, I would need to go to the National Archives to retrieve it all.

Call it luck, paranoia, or just good old-fashioned doubt that the U.S. government was being honest; I did not believe them. I continued the hunt for UFO-related records using the FOIA. Now before I dive into proof of their lies about Project Blue Book, I would like to point out that this is a prime example of one of the challenges when using the FOIA. Even though you might file a FOIA request to the U.S. Air Force, that agency has multiple components, branches, and offices under that particular branch of the military. Meaning, you might decide that the Air Force is the best place to file for your specific request—but then you have to decide which component of the Air Force to file it to. If you do not file it to the right place, you might get a response that says they have "no records" pertaining to your request—but the problem is you just misdirected your letter. Seem confusing? It is.

This is why I filed a FOIA request to WPAFB, in addition to the Head-quarters of the Air Force when seeking UFO documentation. Even though the USAF HQ had already denied my request, I was hoping that WPAFB may have some documentation to give me, since they served as the "home" for Project Blue Book investigations, and maybe some records were left there untapped by researchers.

When I filed this request to WPAFB for UFO records back in 1996, I was again given the same "fact sheet" on Project Blue Book. I was told again that the entire collection of records pertaining to the project was in the possession of NARA, and they had "no records" to give me. In other words, they were just repeating themselves, over and over. The only difference was the letterhead the denial was printed on.

This response coincided with nearly every other request I had sent out to various U.S. Air Force components up until this point, so I was forced to assume they were telling me the truth. That was a huge mistake on my part. This, as I would soon learn, was an outright lie.

A couple years after I received WPAFB's denial along with another copy of the "fact sheet," I happened to pick up a copy of *UFO Magazine*. In this particular issue, there was a small reference to "new UFO documents" being released by the Air Force. I was surprised to read that it was actually WPAFB itself that had released the nearly one thousand pages on Projects Sign and Grudge—the exact topic of my previous request. Yet despite me already seeking the records years prior—and I was told there was nothing there—now I read that nearly one thousand pages were just released. What floored me over all else was that it was the same technical sergeant who signed my denial letter a few years prior that was responsible for releasing these newly found records. The *same* person!

How can in one letter, this person tells me they have no UFO records, then within a couple years, he is the sole person responsible for declassifying and releasing the exact UFO records I was told did not exist? That did not make sense to me, so where did these records come from?

It should be known, that under the FOIA, agencies are required to conduct these searches for records relating to a particular request. This is not a courtesy or a favor, but rather, it is a requirement mandated by law. One could argue that maybe the FOIA officer did not want to look for it or wrongfully assumed there were no records so chose not to conduct a search at all or he simply just did not look hard enough. Regardless of what really happened, all of these explanations go against the true spirit of the FOIA and how the law is written. Although mistakes can absolutely occur, the U.S. government and military was not off to a good start by proving they were taking UFO FOIA requests seriously, or even being honest in the responses I received.

As a result of reading about these newly found records, I re-filed a FOIA request. I directed it to the same officer who signed my original denial letter, the same person who was responsible for releasing these UFO reports mentioned by *UFO Magazine*. Written within my request, I also sought an answer to why my previous case that I filed yielded a "no records" response.

This chain of events displays one of the worst shortcomings to the FOIA, and that is, that no government agency or military department is required to answer *any* question regarding anything. Rather, they are required only to search for records you ask for and then give you the results. This also proves they cannot be held accountable for lying. They can tell you anything they want, and when you can prove beyond any shadow of a doubt they were lying, it does not matter to them. They will not answer anything, nor will they give you an explanation, as their next move proved.

WPAFB sent me a response to that request for these new records, and it was simply a bill to purchase the documents. They gave no explanation on why they were overlooked under my original request. Under the FOIA, agencies are allowed to recover duplication costs beyond the first one hundred pages. Fees vary from agency to agency, and also it depends on the "fee category" you fit in as defined in the FOIA itself, so their bill to obtain the records was, sadly, not out of the ordinary—and it was within their rights spelled out in the law.

Once I paid the fees, I received the nearly one thousand records into my mailbox. These documents were said to not exist—yet here they were. I realized at this moment that my journey exploring the connection between UFOs and the U.S. government was not going to be easy. Under the FOIA, agencies needed to search for records, but as evidenced with this one case, things may not always turn out the way the law intended. This FOIA case also showed that agencies would not follow the rules when it came to conducting a search for responsive documents to a particular request. The writing was on the wall—I had my work cut out for me.

Once I was able to sit down and dissect this new batch of records, and I combined them with other Project Blue Book–related documents I had already received, a pattern quickly emerged. Project Blue Book, on the surface, was touted as that final investigation that concluded UFOs were not real, they were not alien, and, given enough time and evidence, each case could be adequately explained. That is the U.S. government and military's nutshell explanation for all things UFO. That is, as I will prove yet again, only true if you do not look at the actual evidence.

Once you do, their "company line" begins to crumble.

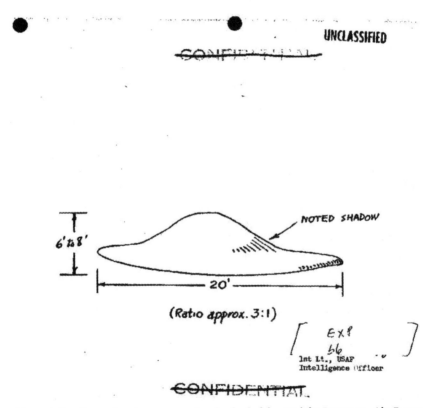

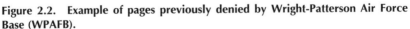

Figure 2.2. Example of pages previously denied by Wright-Patterson Air Force Base (WPAFB).

THE PROJECT BLUE
BOOK DILEMMA

Just like Roswell, the Project Blue Book explanation crumbles once actual documents begin to emerge. Based on the "fact sheet" and subsequent responses to me by the National Archives and Records Administration (NARA), the Project Blue Book collection alone comprises more than forty-two cubic feet of documents within their collection. NARA also states that each cubic foot of records numbers about two thousand pages in length, so with this formula, there are approximately eighty-four thousand pages within the Project Blue Book collection at NARA.

After two decades of utilizing the FOIA, I have learned the U.S. government has more information on *everything* than I can ever properly explain in words. But this may not necessarily be a good thing. If the government buries the public in documents, many of which are meaningless, repetitive, or useless, it may take years, or even decades, to sift through everything the government releases on a particular topic.

For example, take the 2017 and 2018 releases of the previously withheld documents on the JFK assassination. The public waited decades for these documents to see the light of day. Many believed that once released, they would hold the key to unraveling the real mystery behind the events that unfolded on November 22, 1963.

Yet, once the documents were released, the public was buried in hundreds and hundreds of thousands of pages of records. Although this sounds like a good thing, it will take years, if not more than a decade or two, to properly sift through them in an attempt to dissect the truth.

The Project Blue Book collection is a prime example of just that. The U.S. government claims this study solved the riddle behind UFOs, and they pile on tens of thousands of pages to prove it. Though I often wonder: when they officially released these documents to the public a couple decades ago, did they actually think anyone would read them? I ask this because once you do look at the evidence, the "company line" explanation on UFOs and the Project Blue Book "conclusion" simply fall apart.

To the credit of the U.S. Air Force, they realized during their UFO investigations that the military brass heading the projects could not truly grasp the science behind what they were doing. They were brilliant military officers and strategists, but they were not PhDs, scientists, or physicists. Knowing that, they brought in those from various fields of science in order to make sense of the eyewitness accounts, photographs, and film reels that they were beginning to collect. The most prominent, and the most documented in the files, is Dr. J. Allen Hynek.

Dr. Hynek was a well-respected professor and astronomer asked by the U.S. Air Force to join in the beginning days of their UFO research during Project Sign. Throughout those early years, Dr. Hynek acted primarily as a debunker and a skeptic toward the UFO phenomenon. With every case that would cross his desk, he would have some type of "earthly" explanation for it and would put it into the "solved" category.

During Project Sign and Project Grudge, and even into the Project Blue Book era, Dr. Hynek labeled cases as being nothing more than "swamp gas" or the "Planet Venus," and he often used other fallback explanations for the cases they were receiving. Everything seemed to be progressing. UFO cases were being explained, and the scientific approach seemed to be working—that is, until a huge problem for the military began to emerge.

As a scientist evaluating the evidence, Dr. Hynek began to turn from being a debunker and skeptic into a full-fledged believer. The testimonies, the photographs, and the film reels he was analyzing began to convince him that not only were UFOs real, they were not being adequately explained. His fallback explanations were no longer cutting it, and the military's ability to explain almost everything began to fail.

One case that is believed to have turned Dr. Hynek into a believer was the 1964 UFO encounter in Socorro, New Mexico. The witness was a police officer by the name of Lonnie Zamora. The case is still considered an "unknown" and is described in great detail within the Project Blue Book files:

On April 24, 1964, a Socorro, New Mexico policeman, Mr. Lonnie Zamora, reported sighting an object about a mile south of the town at approximately 5:45

p.m., in an unpopulated area full of hills and gullies and covered with sagebrush. Following is a summary of his report to Air Force investigators:

Mr. Zamora reported that while chasing a speeding car north on US 85, he heard a roar and saw flames in an area where a dynamite shack was known to be located. He abandoned chase of the auto and proceeded to where he believed an explosion had occurred. After traveling a little-used road and experiencing considerable difficulty in trying to drive his car up a gravel-covered hill, he said he observed what he thought was an overturned car standing on end. At this point he was about 800 ft. distant from the object and his car was at the crest of a hill with the object ahead of him in a gully. He reported that during this first glance he saw one or two figures in coveralls whom he assumed to be occupants of the object. This is the only time he saw these figures; he did not see them again. After radioing to Police Headquarters at Socorro that he was proceeding to investigate what he believed to be an auto accident, he drove to a point about 150 ft from the gully where the object rested and stopped the car to proceed on foot. He said the object was white, egg or oval-shaped and apparently supported on girderlike legs. He said he heard a roar and saw smoke and flame coming from the bottom of the object. At this point, Mr. Zamora believed that the object was about to explode and he became frightened, turned, and ran to shield himself behind the police car, bumping his leg and losing his glasses on the way. He said that he crouched down, shielding his eyes with his arm while the noise stopped and he glanced up. He reported that the object had risen to a point about 15–20 feet above the ground and the flame and smoke had ceased. At this point, he reported, he noted a design on the object which he described as markings in red about 1 to 1 1/2 ft in height, shaped like a crescent with a vertical arrow and horizontal line underneath. He stated that the object remained stationary for several seconds and then flew off in a southerly direction following the contour of the gully.

Within moments afterward, Sgt Chavez of the New Mexico State Police arrived on the scene in response to Mr. Zamora's earlier radio call. He observed no object, but he reported that there were some slight depressions in the ground and apparently burned brush in the area where Mr. Zamora had reported seeing the object. The brush was cold to the touch. Sgt Chavez reported the incident to local military authorities who conducted the initial investigation.

The Air Force sent investigators from their project office at Wright-Patterson AFB, Ohio. The investigation disclosed the following facts:

No other witnesses to the object reported by Mr. Zamora could be located.

There were no unidentified helicopters or aircraft in the area.

Observers at radar installations had observed no unusual or unidentified blips.

There was no unusual meteorological activity; no thunderstorms. The weather was windy but clear.

There was no evidence of markings of any sort in the area other than the shallow depressions at the location where Mr. Zamora reported sighting the object.

Figure 3.1. Official Project Blue Book photographs of the burned brush and vegetation at the site of the Socorro crash.

Laboratory analysis of soil samples disclosed no foreign material or radiation above normal for the surrounding area.

Laboratory analysis of the burned brush showed no chemicals which would indicate a type of propellant.

This case is considered one of the best within the Project Blue Book collection. Not only did it convince Dr. Hynek that more needed to be done with UFO investigations, it also showed the crucial need for physical evidence when it came to UFO encounters.

As indicated by the files, Officer Zamora witnessed burn marks on the ground, along with impressions that some type of physical craft had landed. Testimony alone tells a great story, but the physical evidence left behind by whatever this craft was proved that this topic had a physical aspect to it and not everything was swamp gas, a planet, or a hallucination.

In 1972, Dr. Hynek wrote and published his book entitled *The UFO Experience: A Scientific Inquiry*, where he shed new light on the true intentions to the U.S. military's UFO research. He repeatedly referenced what he believed to be the biggest problem—and that was the Air Force belief that "it can't be; therefore, it isn't."

Dr. Hynek believed this theorem was the root of the military's expectation for him to debunk rather than truly research. And that is exactly what he did for many years, before the evidence became too convincing to him. To anyone with a scientific background (or to anyone that just wants to use some common sense), this will not give you a credible scientific method or valid conclusion. It appeared that Dr. Hynek was hinting in his book that the military just assumed from the start that UFOs weren't real—and they would do anything to prove it. Their minds were already made up about what the UFO phenomenon really was. This puts forth my theory that Project Blue Book was not a true *investigation*, but rather, it was simply an *explanation*.

These assumptions and faulty investigative methods skewed the statistics. In the end, the final numbers as indicated by the "fact sheet" said that there were 12,618 sightings reported to Project Blue Book, of which only 701 remained "unidentified." Yet, based on the information written by Dr. Hynek after the close of Project Blue Book, we can safely say that these statistics are not accurate nor are they scientific.

Many authors have written about Project Blue Book and dissected case after case, and truly, this era does deserve its own book in itself. Studies by these independent researchers have scoured the Project Blue Book files and have put up a convincing argument that the number of "unknowns" is much higher than the U.S. military has led us to believe.

I have never understood why the scientific community and the general public have just blindly accepted these numbers, results, and final conclusions set forth by the U.S. military. There were still a somewhat large number of "unknown" cases even just dealing with the skewed U.S. military numbers. Why ignore this fact? Although some cases lacked evidence and will never be solved, others had ample evidence like the Socorro case, which are simply discounted to pave the way for the whole "UFOs aren't real" conclusion.

To prove my point on why this is a detriment to true scientific research, I will juxtapose the U.S. military's "UFO investigation" to the pursuit for a cure for cancer. When pursuing a cure for cancer, if you tried 12,618 experiments and 701 of them showed evidence of being a cure, would you just give up because it was only 701 out of 12,618 that showed promise? Would you abandon all scientific studies on a cure for cancer because only 5.56 percent of the time it showed a potential promising result? Of course not—because that's science.

The public largely accepts the U.S. government's request that we should ignore all UFO cases that showed promise simply because a lot of the others were explainable. None of that makes sense, but that's what *they* want you to believe.

Although I only showed one case thus far from the Blue Book files, anyone can see that there is something more to the UFO phenomenon. This one case convinced the primary scientific advisor, Dr. Hynek, to come out of the Project Blue Book investigations and begin his own private organization that would tackle the mystery. He called it the Center for UFO Studies (CUFOS).

That fact in itself shows that the information gathered by Project Blue Book did not solve the mystery. Dr. Hynek was a firm debunker and skeptic, but the evidence they gathered turned him into a believer.

So what went wrong? What happened with what was supposed to be a scientific study into the phenomenon?

Documents that detail a secret 1953 Central Intelligence Agency (CIA) meeting may prove beyond a doubt that this scientific investigation ultimately referred to as Project Blue Book was nothing more than a charade.

INVESTIGATION OR
EXPLANATION?

As we only scratch the surface of Project Blue Book, we realize that despite the U.S. government claim of solving the mystery, Project Blue Book's chief scientific advisor Dr. J. Allen Hynek was not convinced. Rather, he came out of his tenure as an Air Force consultant and began his own private push for the scientific study of UFOs. But why was Project Blue Book ultimately such a failure as a scientific investigation?

A January 1953 committee formed by the CIA may shed some light on answering this question. It was headed by mathematician and physicist Howard P. Robertson, and subsequently, it was called the "Robertson Panel." In addition to Robertson, the panel included: Samuel A. Goudsmit, a nuclear physicist from the Brookhaven National Laboratories; Luis Alvarez, a high-energy physicist; Thornton Page, the deputy director of the Johns Hopkins Operations Research Office and an expert on radar and electronics; and Lloyd Berkner, a director of the Brookhaven National Laboratories and a specialist in geophysics.

These distinguished members of the scientific community were convened in this "secret" panel after a flurry of sightings occurred over Washington, D.C., in the summer of 1952. UFOs were seen over the White House, the Capitol Building, and other sensitive areas during this time, and they lacked any reasonable explanation. It is my opinion that these events were the turning point within the military and the upper echelons of the government that proved the UFO phenomenon was a true threat. This panel was then convened to figure out what to do with the issue that was gaining momentum within the general public.

There were more headlines, more witness reports, and more photographic evidence after the summer of 1952 than ever before. The people of America came to the realization that this phenomenon, these unknown craft, could move

DO NOT RELEASE FROM
ASO/W-A

~~SECRET~~
~~Security Information~~

REPORT OF MEETINGS OF SCIENTIFIC ADVISORY PANEL

ON UNIDENTIFIED FLYING OBJECTS

CONVENED BY OFFICE OF SCIENTIFIC INTELLIGENCE, CIA

January 14 - 18, 1953

25X1A

~~SECRET~~
~~Security Information~~

Declassified by ___006687___
date __2 1 JAN 1975__

49

Figure 4.1. Declassified cover page to the official Robertson Panel Report, formerly classified SECRET.

in and out of the most sensitive airspaces the United States had, with no repercussions. This caused fear and panic within communities around the nation.

In one letter from 1952, which I discovered under FOIA at the Air Force Historical Research Agency (AFHRA), was written by U.S. Air Force Major General William F. Mckee. I discovered this letter while going through his personal records at the archives, and this was not part of any official collection of UFO-related records. It was simply by chance that I realized the letter was there, and it expressed Major General's Mckee's reaction to the 1952 UFO craze. The letter, in part, stated:

> Things are as hectic in Washington as ever. In addition to all of our other troubles, the flying saucer boom has started again. Even our radars are picking up unidentified objects. The press now thinks we are keeping a big secret from them. As General Twining said a day or so ago, people don't seem to realize that we have a few billion stars in the sky with all of their associated physical phenomena.

I have struggled with exactly what the general meant by "their associated physical phenomena," but it was clear that in 1952, the UFO issue was a problem for the military's upper echelon. This letter proved that it was, and it was written at a time when the Cold War with the Soviet Union was heating up. It was just over a decade since the bombing of Pearl Harbor, and the public was worried that another attack on U.S. soil was imminent. Alien or not, the UFO phenomenon was posing a huge problem.

It was the job of the Robertson Panel to evaluate all of the information and data that Projects Sign, Grudge, and Blue Book had collected up until that point, and they needed to determine what to do next. According to their official report, they concluded the following:

> The evidence presented on Unidentified Flying Objects shows no indication that these phenomena constitute a direct physical threat to national security.

The report goes on to state:

> The continued emphasis on the reporting of these phenomena does, in these parlous times, result in a threat to the orderly functioning of the protective organs of the body of politic.

They then recommended

> that the national security agencies take immediate steps to strip the Unidentified Flying Objects of the special status they have been given and the aura of mystery they have unfortunately acquired.

It is with this statement that I believe the true "scientific research" of what Project Blue Book was trying to conduct was thrown out. Dr. Hynek was present for the entire panel and presented to the group members his findings during his time on the projects.

Keep in mind, this was 1953, and Dr. Hynek had not had his epiphany that the UFO topic deserved closer scrutiny. It is argued he was already showing signs of a shift in belief at this point, but that change within him was gradual and slow. It was not until about seven years later, when Dr. Hynek began making public statements in the early 1960s, when it was apparent he began to believe that the UFO phenomenon was real.

To me, the statements and conclusions by the Robertson Panel solidified a single objective for the U.S. Air Force to carry out—and that was to debunk. As indicated by the Robertson Panel report, there was no "national security threat" posed by the UFO phenomenon. Rather, they concluded the true threat to national security was the general public itself. With the fear and hysteria that was rising, the Robertson Panel knew that they needed to dispel the myth behind what UFOs really were; they needed to calm their nerves; and they essentially needed to debunk the UFO phenomenon.

Once they were able to achieve that goal—the public would go away and they would stop asking questions. This appears to be the beginning of the real cover-up. If the Robertson Panel concluded what they did in 1953, then why continue the project for another sixteen years? The only conclusion that makes sense is that the goal of calming down the general public had not been met yet. They knew that they needed to adequately show a large number of "explained" sightings to ultimately solve the mystery and make the public buy it completely.

So how do you skew the scientific results and make sure the UFO investigation never sees anything good? That's easy—just don't give any of the investigators the good stuff.

The discovery of this October 20, 1969, "Department of the Air Force, Air Staff Summary Sheet" with the title "Unidentified Flying Objects (UFO)" and signed by Brigadier General Carroll H. Bolender gives you all the proof you need to prove just that.

The document was obtained by researcher Robert Todd in 1978, and it puts a nail in the coffin when it comes to determining the true scientific nature of the Project Blue Book studies. It states:

> As early as 1953, the Robertson Panel concluded "that the evidence presented on Unidentified Flying Objects shows no indication that these phenomena constitute a direct physical threat to national security" (Atch 9). In spite of this

DEPARTMENT OF THE AIR FORCE AIR STAFF SUMMARY SHEET

					FCC	Coord	
2	AFRDC	Appr		7	SAFRD	Coord	
3	SAFOI	Coord --	Holme	8	SAFOS	Sig	
4	SAFLL	Coord	GIRAUDO	9			
5	AFCCS	Appr		10			

SURNAME OF ACTION OFFICER AND GRADE	SYMBOL	PHONE	TYPIST'S INIT.	SUSPENSE DATE
Major Espey 45-47	AFRDDG	52181	vc	

SUBJECT	DATE
Unidentified Flying Objects (UFO)	20 OCT 1969

SUMMARY

1. For more than twenty years the Air Force has had the responsibility within the Department of Defense for the investigation of unidentified flying objects (UFOs) (Atch 2). As stated in Project Blue Book, this investigative program has two objectives:

    a. To determine whether UFOs pose a threat to the security of the United States; and

    b. To determine whether UFOs exhibit any unique scientific information or advanced technology which could contribute to scientific or technical research (Atch 3)

Procedures for Project Blue Book reporting are defined in Air Force Regulation 80-17. This regulation requires the Commander of an Air Force base to provide a UFO investigative capability and for Air Force Systems Command to continue Project Blue Book (Atch 4). In response to this regulation most Commanders have appointed a UFO investigating officer, usually as an additional duty. Project Blue Book has two officers, one NCO, and one civilian assigned on a full-time basis. In addition, Dr. A. J. Hynek served as a scientific consultant until 1 July 1969.

2. In 1966 the Air Force Office of Scientific Research contracted to have the university of Colorado conduct an independent scientific investigation of unidentified flying objects. This study, directed by Dr. Edward U. Condon and made available as the "Scientific Study of Unidentified Flying Objects," serves as a basis for evaluating the Air Force investigative effort (Atch 5). After an extensive study of this report as well as the review of the report by a panel of the National Academy of Sciences, past studies, Project Blue Book operations and other inputs, the Office of Aerospace research concluded, and we agree, that the continuation of Project Blue Book cannot be justified, either on the ground of national security or in the interest of science (Atch 6).

3. The general conclusion of the Scientific Study of Unidentified Flying Objects is that "nothing has come from the study of UFOs in the past 21 years that has added to scientific knowledge." As to what the federal government should do with the UFO reports it receives from the general public, the authors add that they are "inclined to think that nothing should be done with them in the expectation that they are going to contribute to the advance of science." A panel of the National Academy of Sciences concurred in these views, and the Air Force has found no reason to question this

AF FORM 50 PREVIOUS EDITIONS OF THIS FORM ARE OBSOLETE.

032747

Figure 4.2. The first page of the "Bolender Memo."

finding, the Air Force continued to maintain a special reporting system. There is still, however, no evidence that Project Blue Book reports have served any intelligence function (Atch 8). Moreover, reports of unidentified flying objects which could affect national security are made in accordance with JANAP 146 or Air Force Manual 55-11, and are not part of the Blue Book system (Atch 10). The Air Force experience therefore confirms the impression of the University of Colorado researchers "that the defense function could be performed within the framework established for intelligence and surveillance operations without the continuance of a special unit such as Project Blue Book."

Did you catch the key part of this? "Not part of the Blue Book system"? If the UFO phenomenon does display advanced, even extraterrestrial technology, needless to say that would affect national security at the highest levels. So this document proves that the real cases, those that did show advanced technology, alien or not, were funneled through a different system entirely. In the end, the Project Blue Book investigators never saw these critical cases. I think anyone can conclude at this point that there is no scientific merit to the "investigation" at all if you decide to hide crucial evidence.

Since the closure of Project Blue Book, we have had to rely on the re-cords that were salvaged and housed at the National Archives and Records Administration (NARA). Literally tens of thousands of pages exist there, and although many researchers have scoured these boxes of "unclassified" material (including myself), we can assume much of the material was lost, misplaced, or destroyed. The remains are largely just the case files, but what you don't find are the administrative records, the communications between agencies and the discussions of what was really going on behind the scenes.

As I explained earlier in this book, despite what the U.S. government claims with their "fact sheet," I am able to prove that UFO documents were not all at NARA. Rather, they could be lost somewhere in the bowels of the U.S. government and military's filing systems at the countless offices, subagencies, and archives throughout the nation. E-mails, Microsoft Word, and digital data storage mediums were not available during the Project Blue Book era, so the number of places that miscellaneous documents and material may have ended up is endless.

At this point with Project Blue Book—I had hit a blockade. Since the begin-ning years of my research, I had largely given up on finding "new" material on Project Blue Book, and I focused my investigations elsewhere. Even though I was able to prove otherwise, I was constantly told by the Air Force (and many others) that anything related to UFOs was at NARA, and every request I filed that mentioned Projects Blue Book, Sign, or Grudge or UFOs was automatically rejected and given the "fact sheet" that we have already largely debunked.

That blockade ended for me when a discovery was made deep within a dusty, cob-webbed garage and new documents came to light.

INSIDE THE DESKS OF
PROJECT BLUE BOOK

Although I had concluded early on in my research that Project Blue Book was a farce, I want to explain a story from 2016 that blew my mind. I was producing a television series that was going to mention Project Blue Book for a major network. In the course of my research, I learned about a man by the name of Rob Mercer, an independent researcher from Ohio. He came across the find of a lifetime and discovered something no one else had ever found. His story and background was perfect for my show, and I used it as an excuse to reach out to him and introduce myself.

Mr. Mercer is a history buff and UFO investigator who lives about twenty minutes outside of Wright-Patterson Air Force Base, the previous home of Project Blue Book. He had spent years doing service work inside homes around the Dayton area. He often found himself doing work for former personnel who worked at the base nearby—and even came across some interested in UFOs. Some would have collections of books or binders put together from private investigators, and he would see that these items would eventually be passed on to relatives, who, in most cases, would not care to keep them. He saw many of these collections thrown out into the trash bins, but from time to time, he was able to find items such as these on eBay or similar auction sites for purchase.

One evening in late 2013, while conducting a "UFO" search on Craigslist, Mr. Mercer discovered in the Dayton, Ohio, area that someone had placed an ad for Project Blue Book photographs and documents. It stated that the materials were apparently the property of an Air Force captain who was assigned to Project Blue Book, and they were found behind a pile of lumber bought at auction in a garage in Fairborn, Ohio.

A good portion of Wright-Patterson is located in Fairborn, so upon seeing this, Mr. Mercer was instantly intrigued. There was a good chance that it was the real deal. After reaching out to the one who placed the ad, Mr. Mercer received a response the next morning. He was told that there had been no interest in the files by anyone at that point, so he drove over to look at them. After sifting through the boxes of material, Mr. Mercer was convinced they were authentic, and he purchased the lot. It included slides showing "UFO" photos, briefing documents, two binders with case summaries, full-sized photographs, and various film reels and audio recordings.

After returning home, he began to trace their origin. The seller of the material was not the Air Force officer, but Mr. Mercer was convinced that whoever that was, he was still in the area. He found a name that was on many of the later documents and began his search for a Lt. Carmon Marano. He was able to determine the name he found was associated with a house that had been sold a few years prior to his discovery of the documents. He drove by the house and saw that there was a two-story garage behind it. He thought this was a perfect place for items to be stored, misplaced, and possibly lost over time.

Mr. Mercer set out to confirm that this was the actual Air Force officer's home and not just someone else that shared the same name. He tracked down where Lt. Marano had moved to, and he tried to figure out the best way to approach him. In the case that the military officer was unaware of the files being out, he did not want to expose him to trouble.

Contact was eventually made, and they ended up spending a couple of hours talking. The officer said that he did not realize that he had left the documents behind when he moved out of his previous home. They spoke about his time in the service, the UFO program, and the politics that went with all of that.

After forty-five years, his memory was a little fuzzy, but he remembered some of the cases and recounted the details to Mr. Mercer. The officer said he grew up a fan of science fiction and mentioned that when he was first assigned to the program, he planned to prove that we were being visited by aliens. After two years, he became burned out and convinced otherwise.

When looking at some of the hoaxes and other photos submitted to Project Blue Book, along with the amount of paperwork that went into each case, it is easy to see why this would happen. By the late 1960s, little resources and staff were available, and those that did investigate cases were overworked, tired, and, as Lt. Marano said, "burned out."

His duties included briefings on UFOs for the Air Force and investigating sightings. During his time, he was also charged with organizing case files. Project Blue Book did not have the best relationship with the press, and from time to time, the U.S. Air Force would get requests about specific cases. He took it upon himself to make that process friendlier, and as a result, he would copy case files and organize them into books to make research easier for the media.

After seeing how much Mr. Mercer enjoyed the subject, the officer informed him that he had a few more boxes from his Project Blue Book days stored where he spends spring and summer. Lt. Marano sent Mr. Mercer four more boxes of unclassified material, including books, photos, case files, memos, rules and regulations, film, reel-to-reel sound tape, correspondences, and much more. The files that were acquired included some originals and some copies that were used for the press, and they included investigation tools, books, and other UFO-related documents and interoffice memos from their actual desks. They were earmarked for the trash, but the officer kept them as souvenirs.

When Mr. Mercer told me this story, I was beyond intrigued. The content of those boxes is something that has an immense value to UFO research. By the description alone, I could tell right off the bat that the material he acquired through an ad on Craigslist included records that the general public had never seen before.

I began working with Mr. Mercer to take his collection, which he digitized, and organize it into an online database. As Mr. Mercer digitized the records and sent them over to put onto The Black Vault, I realized that there was much more to these records than I originally thought.

Within the files were previously undiscovered gems from the Project Blue Book era. Many of the letters of correspondence and papers that Lt. Marano had kept as souvenirs never made it into the official Project Blue Book collection at NARA. I believe that some of these papers have no copies, are the originals, and are available nowhere else.

In one particular folder, there were reference cards that were utilized by the Project Blue Book officers to deal with various questions from the public or that allowed them to have a quick reference to particular topics. These cards included quick references that officers could use to respond to certain cases. In other words, it appeared to be a "go to" explanation book to debunk UFO cases.

These cards held explanations for meteors, satellites, and hot air balloons, along with standard responses for sightings more than ninety days old, the George Adamski photographs, and even a standard response to a witness questioning what direction the UFO was traveling during their experience. These cards offered a glimpse into the standard, textbook responses that officers had worked out as the years went on. Another card of interest outlined the views on UFOs by the ranking officer of the Project Blue Book Investigation at the time, Major Hector Quintanilla. This card stated:

UFOs exist in reports only and we have never been able to recover any hardware from an alleged flying saucer. There is absolutely no evidence which would indicate that these alleged saucers were vehicles from another planet or that they were under the guidance of some alien being.

Scientifically, the closest star that could sustain life as you and I know it, is 4 1/2 light years away. That is to say, that if this vehicle left his star and traveled at the speed of light which is 186,000 miles per second, then it would take him nine years to make a round trip. Now thinking a little bit further, we know that anything which has mass/weight cannot travel at the speed of light, so we have to add a few more years to his travel time. There are many, many more problems which have to be taken into consideration, but unfortunately my other duties do not permit the time to explain them fully.

I believe that astronomers in their observatories and the tracking stations throughout the world will detect the presence of a so-called interstellar space vehicle long before it reaches our earth's envelope. If such an event ever occurs, then these gentlemen would have notified the world long before you and I could detect them with the naked eye. I honestly don't believe that these learned gentlemen of science would keep such an event to themselves and not reveal it to the general public. After all, fame and fortune await the discoverer of such an event.

"Gentlemen of science"? These cards also gave an interesting look at the viewpoints on the opposite sex in the 1950s and 1960s, but that is another book in itself. So I will leave that one alone. You can see, however, the views of Major Quintanilla were already decided, and the "scientific" inquiry that he headed within the U.S. Air Force seemed to already have had a conclusion drawn and was fairly closed-minded to any result other than the desired "UFOs aren't real" standard response.

Another batch of letters was from the official correspondence files of Dr. J. Allen Hynek. These were letters back and forth between himself and Major Quintanilla. One particular letter expressed Dr. Hynek's disappointment that Project Blue Book was seemingly ignoring the good cases. In this November 20, 1967, letter, Dr. Hynek inquires why one particular case from Saigon was seemingly left out of Project Blue Book altogether:

Dear Major Quintanilla:
As reported, this case is completely unidentified and much additional information is called for. It is inconceivable that military intelligence would not have looked further into this case and, therefore, I should like to request that any further information garnered in this case be forwarded to Project Blue Book.

It goes on to state:

Since the source of this information was himself a member of a military intelligence detachment, it appears all the more incomprehensible that this incident was not followed up in considerable detail.

Dr. Hynek also expressed his disagreement with the official explanation that some UFO cases received. He went on the record to say he felt some of these cases needed a second evaluation and the "conclusion" that Project Blue Book labeled on them was false. Another letter from Dr. Hynek, dated November 17, 1967, also to Major Quintanilla, stated:

On re-examination, I find no substantiation for the evaluation of hoax, particularly in view of the photo analysis report, No. 67-10, dated 20 February 1967, which contains no information upon which a hoax can be based. To the contrary, the report states that close examination of the negative has negated double exposure and/or retouching. The photographs appear genuine insofar as content is concerned; however, no satisfactory explanation of the unidentified object could be made. The lack of a satisfactory explanation of the unidentified object does not constitute sufficient reason to declare it a hoax. Further, the interviewer considered the witness to be a "reliable source."

Major Quintanilla received a promotion to lieutenant colonel toward the end of Project Blue Book, and in 1968, he was not quiet about his disagreements with Dr. Hynek. One particular letter he wrote to Dr. Hynek was dated October 11, 1968:

I have just read the "Electronic News" article of September 30, 1968, with regards to the National Electronics Conference panel on UFOs. The article states that you and three other gentlemen will appraise the current status of UFOs and review the latest findings, including those of the Condon committee. I wish to inform you that under no circumstances will you review the findings of the Condon Committee as an official Air Force Consultant. The review of the findings of the Condon committee will be under taken by the National Academy of Sciences; therefore, the Air Force is not going to involve itself with Dr Condon's report until the National Academy releases the document to the Secretary of the Air Force and the general public.

2. As your project monitor, I would appreciate it if you would refrain from identifying yourself as an Air Force consultant when participating in pseudo-scientific panels of this type.

HECTOR QUINTANILLA, Jr, Lt Colonel, USAF

This gave an inside look at the tone from the upper brass toward Dr. Hynek, as he began to branch out and take part in valid UFO research within the private sector. This probably stemmed from Dr. Hynek expressing his strong disagree-ments with Project Blue Book erroneously labeling cases as "solved" or a "hoax."

The reference Lt. Col. Quintanilla made to "pseudo-scientific panels" also shows the mindset that he was in when it came to the UFO phenomenon. For him to label scientific panels as such showed an extreme disrespect and lack of appreciation for the field of study. It also disregards the conclusions that their own scientific advisor had made after looking at the evidence. These letters prove that the writing was on the wall—Dr. Hynek was rogue, and he no longer was helping with the "company line."

Mr. Mercer's find included much more than just these inside looks into correspondence files of Dr. Hynek. Lt. Marano had salvaged a large batch of reference material that the staff used during their investigations. This included books, reference material on some of their commonly used UFO explanations (like clouds, meteors, and satellites), and even a small batch of the original case files and reports from the Blue Book investigations.

At quick glance, these individual case files may be dismissed by seasoned UFO investigators because they appear to be nearly identical to what was in the public collection within NARA. However, upon closer examination, this is not true. The collection Mr. Mercer acquired had more never-before-seen case files that do not exist at NARA—and they told an amazing story. These files, which mysteriously disappeared when the Project Blue Book collection was compiled at NARA, show the true mindset of the investigators in the field.

When cases came in to Project Blue Book, they did not have the staff within their offices to fly their investigators throughout the nation to investigate. Rather, they enlisted the help of regionally located military officers to do a proper investigation. At least, "proper" was the intent.

One example from these newly acquired files was from a UFO sighting that occurred on July 1, 1969. The witness was from WPFA, a local radio station, and he described his sighting as a "silver colored, cone-shaped object with negative sound [that] was stationary at 1,500' over the Town and Country Shopping Center, next to the radio station in Pensacola." As a result, word passed to the military, and an investigation ensued.

Project Blue Book enlisted the help of a military officer at Florida's Eglin Air Force Base by the name of Ben Z. M. Gershater. His rank was unknown at the time of the report, but he retired as a major from the U.S. Air Force and passed away in 1980 at the age of sixty-five. After his investigation, he submitted the report to the offices of Project Blue Book located at Wright-Patterson Air Force Base in Ohio. Once you read this, there will be no wonder why this report was "lost" and never made it into the official files at NARA.

The report had the subject line "UFO Report; or: The Credulity, Imbecility, Gullibility and/or Hysteria of Some Jerks of the Current Under-30 Generation." This line alone shows the complete disregard for a witness who decided to come forward about a UFO sighting, even if it was prosaic in nature. It seems, as the evidence piles up, most involved with Project Blue Book had their minds already made up on what UFOs were, even before having taken part in a single investigation. They would just simply blame it on hallucinations or, like in this case, the "stupidity" of the witness—but they did not care about credible evidence or testimony.

Toward the end of this report, Gershater stated:

> The relative humidity, in Pensacola, at the time of yesterday's 1900 UFO sighting may have been only 68%. But the relative stupidity of Mr. ___, and others of his gullible WPFA colleagues, had reached saturation point at 100%.

But he did not stop there—just weeks later, he doubled down on his insults, but this time, it was directed toward two military officers who witnessed a UFO.

On July 22, 1969, two airmen witnessed "a round UFO, white-colored, circular shape of half-dime size, with 'lighted wings' in an inverted-V extending from it, to the ESE. Neither could estimate altitude. They stated that it was generally 'stationary' for the next two (2) hours but occasionally moved slightly to the left, to the right, upwards and downwards, in 90-degree motions, then returning to its position 'beneath, above, or to the edge of a stationary cloud, oval in shape.'"

The same investigator from Eglin Air Force Base, Ben Z. M. Gershater, was dispatched to investigate. In the end, he submitted his report, and he continued

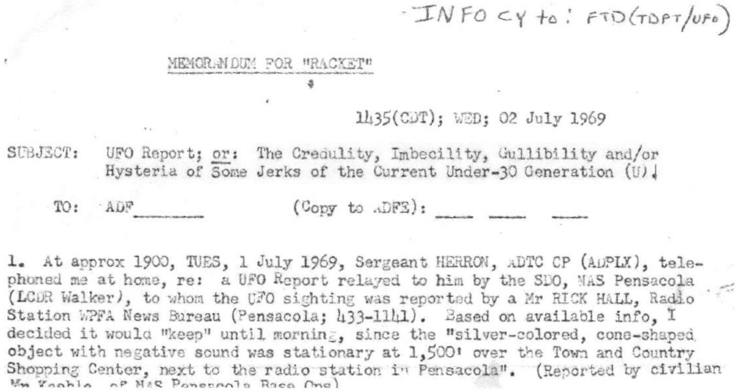
INFO CY to: FTD(TDPT/UFO)

MEMORANDUM FOR "RACKET"

1435(CDT); WED; 02 July 1969

SUBJECT: UFO Report; or: The Credulity, Imbecility, Gullibility and/or Hysteria of Some Jerks of the Current Under-30 Generation (U)

TO: ADF______ (Copy to ADFE): ___ ___ ___

1. At approx 1900, TUES, 1 July 1969, Sergeant HERRON, ADTC CP (ADPLX), telephoned me at home, re: a UFO Report relayed to him by the SDO, NAS Pensacola (LCDR Walker), to whom the UFO sighting was reported by a Mr RICK HALL, Radio Station WPFA News Bureau (Pensacola; 433-1141). Based on available info, I decided it would "keep" until morning, since the "silver-colored, cone-shaped object with negative sound was stationary at 1,500' over the Town and Country Shopping Center, next to the radio station in Pensacola". (Reported by civilian

Figure 5.1. Letterhead of one of the documents, written by Ben Z. M. Gershater, showing the tone and predetermination on UFO cases.

his tone as the subject line read, "UFO Report; or: (Chapter II in Current Credulity, Imbecility, Gullibility and/or Hysteria of the Under-30s (U)."

This time, Gershater felt so strongly that the UFO investigation was a waste of time, he even recommended to the upper brass that anyone who submits UFO reports that are deemed so easily explainable be court-martialed and punished. He also outlined, for the second time, a detailed list of the costs involved with investigating the sighting. He referenced his "7 hours of time, neglecting more important duties and work, on this UFO, including the making of eight (8) long distance telephone calls" all charged to Eglin Air Force Base.

In other words, UFO witnesses were idiots and UFO investigations were a waste of time, resources, and money. Although this was approaching the end of Project Blue Book, these case files, never before seen, highlight the true nature of what Project Blue Book was all about. They seal the deal when it comes to showing that Project Blue Book was nothing of a true *investigation*, but rather, it was simply an *explanation*.

It took many years for me to really dissect Project Blue Book and see that not only was it the root of the "company line" explanation, it was a farce. We can conclude that there really was no science behind this "scientific" investigation, and the material that may actually prove something was funneled somewhere else or maybe even lost completely.

That did not stop me from trying to find more evidence to prove it. Where did these valuable case files end up? It took years of filing FOIA requests, but I uncovered that it was actually every major government agency that had UFO files for me to find. And if you believe the "company line" the U.S. government often touts, nearly every page I received from every agency I went to should not exist.

THE NATIONAL
SECURITY
THREAT BEGINS

Project Blue Book files show the U.S. Air Force attempted to explain every UFO encounter that came across their desk, but their scientific advisor left the project believing they were wrong to dismiss them all. Lost Project Blue Book files found in the garage of a former Air Force officer involved in the program display without a doubt how at least one military officer felt about the "waste of time" that UFO investigations caused. With these facts and the clear disregard for the scientific method, you would think that not much came out of the Project Blue Book files that was of value to UFO research. However, that could not be further from the truth!

Beginning in 1953, the Robertson Panel set forth the notion that the only threat was the general public itself and their interest in UFOs. They ignored quite a few cases that displayed a true threat to national security, and they wanted to maintain that UFOs were explainable and not a threat. This determination set forth by the panel proposed that the citizens of America had the ability to flood the resources of the military with questions and direct requests for answers. It was at that point that I believe the cover-up truly began and the agenda of debunking anything relating to UFOs went into full force.

To the contrary of the Robertson Panel's "conclusion," Project Blue Book files are actually ripe with cases that display a threat to the national security of the United States. This posed a big problem with the military's public relations campaign to dispel the myth behind flying saucers. Keep in mind, when most of the Project Blue Book documents were written and cases were "dismissed" as a weather inversion, the planet Venus, or swamp gas, military personnel never thought their writing would ever enter the public domain. The Freedom of

Information Act (FOIA) was not created until 1967, and even then, it was in its infant stages and was a much different beast than it is now. But since its creation, the FOIA and subsequent releases of documents by the U.S. military have shed a new light on what Project Blue Book was able to find but largely covered up.

Arguably, one of the biggest displays of this true threat to national security occurred right before the Robertson Panel ever convened at the CIA. Some experts believe that these events motivated the Robertson Panel to be convened in the first place. The events that unfolded caused panic throughout the streets.

As evident within the documents that Lt. Carmon Marano kept in his garage for decades, 1952 displayed a severe threat to the national security of the United States that no Air Force investigator could explain. Selfridge Air Force Base, Michigan; Lockbourne Air Force Base, Ohio; Randolf Air Force Base, Texas; Travis Air Force Base, California; Andrews Air Force Base, Washington, D.C.; Kirtland Air Force Base, New Mexico; and Holloman Air Force Base, New Mexico, all had UFO encounters that could not be explained by Project Blue Book investigators, and they remain "unidentified" to this day.

Military bases were "no fly zones" for normal commercial and private air traffic. The only craft that were allowed to fly within these areas were controlled by the military itself. Yet each of these bases was being encroached by unidentified craft, and the military was at a loss trying to figure out who or what they were.

Despite these incursions on sensitive military bases, it was in the skies over Washington, D.C., that the UFO phenomenon proved that it could not be identified nor could it be stopped. From July 12 to July 29, 1952, a large "UFO wave" of sightings was seen throughout the Washington, D.C., area. In fact, in 1952, Project Blue Book saw one of the biggest influx of case reports they had ever seen. This enormous increase would remain the highest number all the way through to the end of their official investigation in 1969. No other year had as high of a number as 1952.

Some of these encounters were chronicled by the official historian of the CIA and the National Reconnaissance Office (NRO), Gerald K. Haines. He wrote in his publication "CIA's Role in the Study of UFOs, 1947–90—A Die-Hard Issue" the following:

> A massive buildup of sightings over the United States in 1952, especially in July, alarmed the Truman administration. On 19 and 20 July, radar scopes at Washington National Airport and Andrews Air Force Base tracked mysterious blips. On 27 July, the blips reappeared. The Air Force scrambled interceptor aircraft to investigate, but they found nothing. The incidents, however, caused headlines across the country. The White House wanted to know what was happening, and

TOTAL UFO SIGHTINGS, 1947 - 1969

YEAR	TOTAL SIGHTINGS	UNIDENTIFIED
1947	122	12
1948	156	7
1949	186	22
1950	210	27
1951	169	22
1952	1,501	303
1953	509	42
1954	487	46
1955	545	24
1956	670	14
1957	1,006	14
1958	627	10
1959	390	12
1960	557	14
1961	591	13
1962	474	15
1963	399	14
1964	562	19
1965	887	16
1966	1,112	32
1967	937	19
1968	375	3
1969	146	1
TOTAL	12,618	701

62- 83894 - 4.83

Figure 6.1.   Breakdown of sightings clearly showing a surge in 1952.

the Air Force quickly offered the explanation that the radar blips might be the result of "temperature inversions." Later, a Civil Aeronautics Administration investigation confirmed that such radar blips were quite common and were caused by temperature inversions.

What Mr. Haines fails to say is that the Project Blue Book files also had numerous sightings throughout the nation by human observers (and not just on radar), which confirmed structured craft of some kind that were flying above them. The absence of this detail by this government report shows that not all evidence is being offered to the public. In other words, the report implied that only radar sightings existed at this time, but in reality, the actual case reports from Project Blue Book involving witnesses of a human nature prove otherwise.

Despite this inconsistency in this particular report, in 1952, this influx of case reports, especially those in July of that year, motivated the Air Force to hold a press conference. They knew the public wanted answers.

So at 4:00 p.m. on July 29, 1952, in Room 3E-869 at the Pentagon, Major General John A. Samford, director of intelligence, U.S. Air Force, sat in a chair to field questions from the media. He attempted to explain away most UFO sightings as being mundane occurrences, but tucked away amid his attempt to debunk the "flying saucer myth," he acknowledged the seriousness of some UFO cases:

> However, there have remained a percentage of this total, in the order of twenty percent of the reports, that have come from credible observers of relatively incredible things. And because of these things not being possible for us to move along and associate with the kind of things that we've found can be associated with the bulk of these reports, we keep being concerned about them.

In addition to this press conference, two days later, Major General Samford recorded a statement on film regarding flying saucers. The film was discovered at NARA and holds the "National Archives Identifier" number 25738 and the "Local Identifier" number 111-LC-30875. The film is five minutes in length and contains snippets of statements about "flying saucers" and details about the Air Force "investigation" into the UFO phenomenon.

Major General Samford repeated many of the statistics and figures from the press conference just days prior, but he also confirmed again the seriousness of the "credible observers" who are seeing "incredible things." What is also interesting from the film reel is that it ends with Major Donald Keyhoe, a Marine Corps Naval aviator. Although Major Keyhoe would go on to found a UFO research organization of his own, at this time, his career was primarily writing for pulp magazines in the 1920s and 1930s and then re-entering service during World War II in a Naval Aviation Training Division.

After World War II, he continued with his UFO interest, and he published the book *Flying Saucers Are Real* in 1950. Toward the end of July 1952, he appeared on this archived film reel after Major General Samford, and his tone was much different from the U.S. Air Force's official statements:

> With all due respect to the Air Force, I believe some of them will prove to be of interplanetary origin. During a three year investigation, I have found that many pilots have described objects of substance and high speed. One case, the pilots reported their plane was buffeted by an object that had passed them at 500 miles an hour. Obviously this was a solid object, and I believe it was from outer space.

Major Keyhoe's opinion was based on years of research, writing various articles, and studying the information that was available at the time. How could an experienced Naval aviator, trained as a pilot, see the UFO evidence and become so convinced that it proved an extraterrestrial connection? Major Keyhoe's experience that brought him to this conclusion spanned far beyond a personal interest. The *New York Times* wrote in their obituary for Major Keyhoe when he died in 1988:

> In the 1920's, Mr. Keyhoe, a pilot with the Marine Corps, accompanied Charles A. Lindbergh in publicity flights across the United States, after Lindbergh's solo flight across the Atlantic.
>
> His interest in unidentified flying objects began in 1949 and he came to believe that they were from outer space. He wrote several books about U.F.O.'s, including *Flying Saucers Are Real* in 1950 and *Flying Saucers from Outer Space* in 1953.

After the press conference, the mystery only deepened. Despite the Air Force's best attempts to squash any interest in the UFO phenomenon, it grew to greater levels within the eyes of the public. Project Blue Book investigators struggled to find explanations for some of the cases they were receiving, and the general public continued to ask questions.

In the end, many explanations put onto UFO cases within the Project Blue Book system were highly criticized by Major Keyhoe, Dr. J. Allen Hynek, and others who scrutinized the Air Force files in the years after Project Blue Book. In fact, back in 2015, I put most of the Project Blue Book documents onto The Black Vault after receiving digital copies of them and organizing them in a way that no one had done before. It was a searchable database by keyword but also could be browsed by the year the UFO sighting took place. It then broke down the locations in the form of cities and states, along with the specific date, if available.

The amount of media attention to this new database I had built was something that quite surprised me. Although, sadly, the story got misrepresented by some major media outlets (they misidentified the files as being "newly released"), the story went global on a scale I was not expecting. I appeared on the *Today* show and *ABC World News Tonight* and did quite a few interviews regarding the records, but many other media outlets never bothered to ask me questions and incorrectly reported the story without ever having me on. Facts are very important to this topic, and this was a prime example of erroneous news coverage that does not help the public better understand what information is really there and how important it really is.

Despite that frustration, in the short time that these files were online, I received quite a few letters from people that had heard or read about this database of Project Blue Book files on The Black Vault. I was amazed that some of the letters I received were from the actual witnesses themselves that had reported their sighting to the Air Force through the 1940s, 1950s, and 1960s. They were able to find their actual reports, based on their own testimony decades prior.

Some found their testimony, while others found their photographs or film reels along with the subsequent investigation by the Air Force. But one thing stuck out from the letters I received—they were all upset at the "conclusion" by the Air Force. In fact, most of them at the time never heard back from the Air Force at all, so they had no idea what they had concluded about the experiences. They gave their reports to the military and did the interviews, but they never heard anything after that. Posting these files online gave these witnesses an opportunity to see how the Air Force treated their cases and what determination they came up with.

On more than one occasion, I received letters that stated they felt the Air Force changed their story so they could put an "explanation" on it. They believed that facts were either omitted or altered so certain explanations could be put onto their case and have it go into the "solved" column.

One letter I received from a witness to a UFO in February of 1969 in Hamburg, New York, was so detailed I want to share it in its entirety. It is done so here with permission, but the witness asked to remain anonymous:

> As a 15 year old teenager, I was always interested in science, especially astronomy, space science and the Apollo program. I habitually set up my Kodak Vigilant camera (100mm / f8.8) using 620 (120mm) film on dark clear nights

in the hopes of capturing a meteor streaking through the night sky. The camera was using ASA 400 black & white verichrome pan film and screwed onto my heavy duty tripod to prevent vibration. I used a 16 inch cable shutter release which had a setscrew. The setscrew could be tightened to keep the lens open for those long-duration photos necessary to capture the meteor streak. After taking pictures of the night sky for a few hours, I developed the film and was absolutely astonished to see the image. Sadly, I never saw what made the strange images. You see . . . I had a habit of setting up, triggering the camera and going inside the house to drink hot coco; reappearing outside every few minutes to stop the camera exposure, wind the film and then continue with my iterative meteor photography. I do not remember there being snow on the ground but I do recall it being cold. You can check the weatherunderground.com historic data base for average temperatures on sunny days/clear nights toward the middle of February and what you'll find is the clear days in February 1968 were averaging +20F. Likewise, a variety of on-line celestial calendars will tell you what phase and location the moon was in the sky. The moon was full around mid-month (February 14) and in crescent phase near the end of the month (February 27).

What's important to note on the two files containing the photograph:

The first case file: A 6 page PDF document consisting of 5 photographs. These are my original submissions consisting of one (1) contact print and four (4) 8inch x 10inch enlargements. Each enlargement varies in exposure time to enhance the star trails and objects. Note the clarity of the photos—the deep blacks and the clean whites. On the last page (p6/6) is a photo of a ball cap labeled "artifact from Florida file1981". I know nothing of this hat and can assume it was erroneously included in the PDF file as a result of the automated PDF processing.

The second case file: A 16 page compilation consisting of my original submission letters, poor duplicates of my original five photographs together with a series of letters between Blue Book personnel and myself answering questions and later my requests for return of all the data.

Although there is only one (1) original negative displaying the unusual objects, I originally submitted four (4) 8inch x 10inch enlargements and one (1) contact print made from that single negative. These enlargements, excellent in quality, vary in exposure time so as to allow more or less detail to be shown. That's why star trails are denser in some of the photographs while others seem to be washed out. The enlargements I originally submitted to Blue Book can be viewed on the first case file. However, in the second case file, the Blue Book letter on the last page states they had analyzed the one (1) 5inch × 7inch print and it was of poor quality. I'm not sure where that one print originated from since I submitted nothing like that. I'm left wondering if Blue Book personnel made a Xerox copy of one of my original enlargements and submitted that "poor" copy to their intelligence analyst for a review.

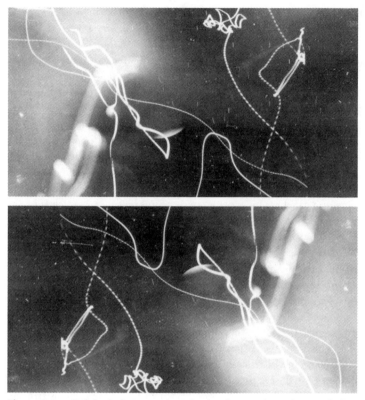

Figure 6.2.   Original photographs submitted to Project Blue Book that the witness feels were doctored.

Near the center of the photo is an oscillating blinking trail. This is an airplane, most likely headed to the Buffalo International airport. The blinking is a result of the normal aircraft strobes. I remember hearing a plane during the time period. I do not recall hearing the distinctive rotor wash of a helicopter. There are also a variety of star-trails shown in the photo. The camera was pointed upward at about a 45 degree angle towards the sky with an azimuth of about 120 degrees (towards the southeast). You can plug the approximate date I took the photograph (mid- to late-February 1968) into just about any modern astronomy program and deduce what the night sky looked like during that time period to verify the actual constellation position, hence the azimuth and elevation of the original photograph. Something else to note are the dimensions of some of the strange objects in question. By knowing the focal length of the camera lens, film dimensions and the size of the image on the negative, an approximate true-size of an object can be determined. This is the basis of photographic analysis. Even as a kid, I realized one of the strange objects in question was approximately 15 feet in diameter. One additional fact I wanted to mention. This photo is only 1 of a 24 photographic sequence I took that night. I was taking photographs for several hours, alternating exposure times to attempt to capture that elusive meteor. The 10 or so photos prior to and the 13 after this particular unusual one showed absolutely nothing odd, just a quiescent night sky and star trails.

Blue Book analysts called these multiple lights "multiple exposure of flashing light source." I think not. This was a clear and cloudless night sky with plenty of continuous star trails within the photograph showing there were no breaks in the camera exposure due to vibration or clouds or movement. Note the continuity, length, and direction of the star trails. The star trails alone are irrefutable photographic evidence of the camera direction, continuous exposure time period and clarity of the night sky. The multiple exposure theory is incredibly absurd. Flashing light source . . . yes, but what was it that was flashing? It appears the strobing light completing the incredible turns is at a timed rate. The erratic aerial pattern suggests something not within our airplane capability but possibly within the realms of a helicopter. Yet even so, why perform flight maneuvers as depicted and at night? As to the other strange light forms especially the one mysterious crescent shaped object near the center of the photograph, it is most baffling to me. Whatever these objects were, they came into the camera field of view, completed their maneuvers and left in a time period not longer than 3 minutes.

I still possess the original 620/120mm film negative, the contact prints, the enlargements I made and the response from the Project Blue Book personnel, all still in the original envelope.

Although I no longer live in Hamburg, I still set up cameras to capture odd things in the night sky. Now-a-days though, I use three (3) Canon digital SLR cameras with large memory cards and electronic timing mechanisms. On clear dark nights here in Alaska, I typically take over 3,000 photos. And yes . . . I still capture plenty of "interesting" things in the night sky although nothing as near fascinating as my 1968 photos.

If I only received this one letter, I would think maybe it was a fluke. However, this was only one of a growing number of e-mails and letters I was receiving. These letters not only supported my theory that Project Blue Book was a farce, but they also introduced a new factor that I did not expect. These letters showed the huge possibility that Project Blue Book, during an era when the FOIA did not exist, was going so far as to fabricate evidence, squash witness testimony, and alter the facts in order to "solve" a case and make it disappear.

There was no doubt that Project Blue Book investigators were faced with a high number of hoaxes, misidentified aircraft, and sightings by citizens of just everyday military aircraft. However, as Major General Samford stated many times throughout his press conferences and recorded statements, there was a percentage of "credible observers" who were seeing "incredible things."

I believe the evidence has now come out, when sifting through the official files of Project Blue Book, to prove the investigation was nothing of the sort. And to continue along that line, I believe that the files also prove there was a large national security threat, not due to the general public asking questions but rather whatever this phenomenon was—it was able to do what it wanted, when it wanted, and where it wanted—and there was nothing the U.S. military could do to stop it.

That is, by definition, a threat to national security. And despite the U.S. government wanting us everyday people to believe that UFO cases and investigations stopped when Project Blue Book closed in 1969, their own evidence proves that not only is that not true—but the threats to national security continued and strengthened as the years went on.

THE NATIONAL
SECURITY
THREAT DEEPENS

Although it takes a small amount of work, dispelling the myth of what I have called the "company line" is quite easy. Although deep down some of you may just assume the government is lying about UFOs (and sometimes that is the best course of action), you can get evidence to *prove* that lie in the form of their own official documentation quite easily.

What I am still amazed by the most, even after decades of researching this, is that the U.S. government will actually freely give you that evidence, even though it completely contradicts their "company line" and what they want you to believe. All you have to do is ask for it.

Once you do, as I have outlined in the previous six chapters, their "scientific investigation" falls apart. They put little to no effort into truly unraveling the mystery, and those that did, like Dr. J. Allen Hynek and Major Donald Keyhoe, came away with a *belief* in the phenomenon, not a *doubt*.

In the final days of Project Blue Book, the U.S. military denounced any interest in the phenomenon, and after this project was closed, they recommended reporting sightings to private UFO research organizations or, if a witness felt so inclined, reporting them to local law enforcement. The bottom line was that their UFO investigation was closed, and the U.S. government and military withdrew any interest in taking in any more sighting reports.

Entwined in this massive misconception about UFOs, the U.S. government and military alike stressed for decades there was "no threat to national security" from the phenomenon. This belief is why they felt the public should lose interest; the military should waste no more time, effort, or money on investigating it;

IMMEDIATE RELEASE .

December 17, 1969   NO. 1077-69
                       OXford 7-5131 (Info.)
                       OXford 7-3189 (Copies)

AIR FORCE TO TERMINATE
PROJECT "BLUE BOOK"

Secretary of the Air Force Robert C. Seamans, Jr., announced
today the termination of Project Blue Book, the Air Force program
for the investigation of unidentified flying objects (UFOs).

In a memorandum to Air Force Chief of Staff General John D. Ryan,
Secretary Seamans stated that "the continuation of Project Blue Book
cannot be justified either on the ground of national security or in
the interest of science," and concluded that the project does not merit
future expenditures of resources.

The decision to discontinue UFO investigations was based on:

- An evaluation of a report prepared by the University of
  Jrado entitled, "Scientific Study of Unidentified Flying Objects."

- A review of the University of Colorado's report by the
National Academy of Sciences.

- Past UFO studies.

- Air Force experience investigating UFO reports during the past
two decades.

Under the direction of Dr. Edward U. Condon, the University of
Colorado completed an 18-month contracted study of UFOs and its report
was released to the public in January, 1969. The report concluded that
little if anything has come from the study of UFOs in the past 21 years
that has added to scientific knowledge, and that further extensive
study of UFO sightings is not justified in the expectation that science
will be advanced.

The University of Colorado report also states that, "It seems that
only so much attention to the subject (UFOs) should be give as the
Department of Defense deems to be necessary strictly from a defense point
of view....It is our impression that the defense function could be
performed within the framework established for intelligence and surveillance operations without the continuance of a special unit such as
'ect Blue Book, but this is a question for defense specialists rather
 ¬ research scientists."

A panel of the National Academy of Sciences made an independent
assessment of the scope, methodology, and findings of the University of

MORE

Figure 7.1.   U.S. Air Force press release terminating Project Blue Book.

and the entire world should believe that the mystery was solved. They wanted everyone to just stop asking questions and simply go away.

There was something that never sat right with me about their "company line." I felt, even when I was fifteen years old, that the entire Project Blue Book story was a cover and the real information was hidden away somewhere else. I realized quickly that there was a big problem to their overall "conclusion" about UFOs they were touting to the public. That problem was that the phenomenon did not go away with the closure of Project Blue Book; it only got worse.

The greatest trick of a magician is to convince the audience to look at their right hand, so they miss what is going on in their left. I studied magic before I did UFOs, and I was fascinated by it all. I felt this one trick alone could absolutely be attributed to a government cover-up, which is precisely the reason I did not believe the "company line" in the first place. I am glad I studied magic before ever becoming interested in UFOs because when it came to this topic, the U.S. government was trying to get away with a complicated parlor trick illusion . . . and I was not buying it for a moment.

This leads me to the story about the first document I ever received under the Freedom of Information Act (FOIA). It might be strange in chapter 7 of this book to jump back to the beginning of *my* journey, but I feel this is an important thing to do. This document obviously holds a special place in my heart for sparking my interest in this field, but these four pages also blew away single-handedly the entire "company line" that the U.S. government and military was handing out.

Now let me say up front, with this document, I do not lay a claim to discovering it. It had been in the "public domain" for a few years prior to me reading it. However, once I did lay eyes on it, I was hooked and had to verify that it was real. And after filing my first FOIA request to get it—I realized it was very real!

It reads like the plot of an opening scene to next summer's blockbuster sci-fi movie or something you might see on an episode of *The X-Files*. But it's neither. Rather, it is an official document that I was able to verify from the Defense Intelligence Agency (DIA), and you will soon see why it started me on my lifelong journey.

The document details a UFO encounter that occurred in 1976, and if you take the U.S. government at their word, the document itself should not even exist in the first place since it was created seven years after Project Blue Book closed. Aside from that major blunder, the information within it displays technology far beyond what was available in 1976, 1986, 1996, 2006, and 2016, and to be blatantly honest, we do not even seem to be on the cusp of exhibiting this type of technology anytime soon.

In the field of UFOlogy, this encounter has become known as the "1976 Iran Incident," and to this day, it remains unexplained. The story, according to this official document, goes like this.

In 1976, in Tehran, Iran, an unidentified object was seen over the city by local residents. This sighting sparked at least four phone calls to the nearest Imperial Iranian Air Force command post, and the senior officer on duty attempted to convince the callers they were simply seeing stars. He did not have any aircraft airborne, and he thought nothing of it.

After the fourth call, however, he became intrigued enough to go outside and see for himself. Sure enough, he witnessed the object, which was much larger and brighter than any star in the sky. He realized he needed to take action.

He scrambled an F-4 Phantom jet to engage this unknown object. While on approach, the pilot reached 24 nautical miles away (27.6 miles) when something bizarre happened. The pilot lost all instrumentation and communication.

As the pilot broke off pursuit of the UFO, he regained it all, so he assumed it was a plane malfunction and returned to base. Ten minutes later, a second F-4 Phantom jet was scrambled to intercept.

Upon reaching the same distance as the first jet of 24 nautical miles, something bizarre happened yet again. This time, the pilot witnessed the UFO begin to move away from his aircraft, keeping a constant distance of 24 nautical miles. The object, according to this document, would move as fast or as slow as it needed to keep that distance of 24 nautical miles exactly.

The document then mentions a second object, which suddenly appeared out of the first UFO that the pilot was attempting to intercept. This second object began to head straight toward the F-4 Phantom at a great rate of speed. To any military pilot, if an object comes off of an aircraft and quickly comes toward you, that's an aggressive maneuver and most likely a missile—so you have to act fast.

The F-4 pilot quickly armed his AIM-9 missile to fire back. As he is ready to fire in 3 . . . 2 . . . 1 . . . everything shuts down. His communications, his instrumentation, it all goes offline, and his attempt to fire back fails.

At this point, he is simply a sitting duck for what he believes is an incoming missile. Yet, before impact, this second UFO makes a turn, loops around his aircraft, and returns to the original UFO for a perfect rejoin. This was clearly not a missile, but what was it?

This story gets even more bizarre. A third UFO now appears out of the original craft. The pilot observes this third UFO descend straight toward the ground also at a great rate of speed, but right before impact, the object simply hovers and casts a light approximately one-and-a-half to two miles in diameter over the area.

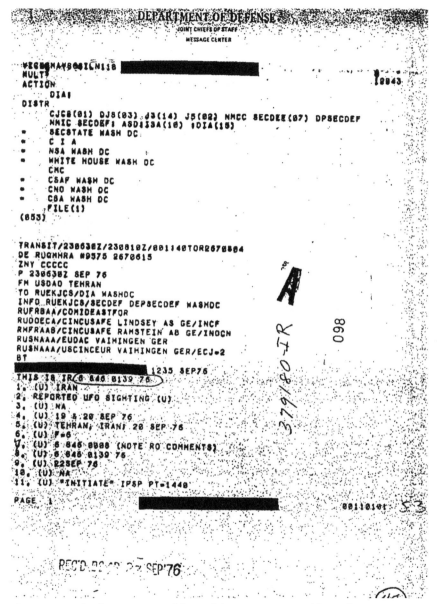

```
VZCZCNAYS001LN118
MULT?                                                              [8843
ACTION
      DIA1
DISTR
      CJCS(01) DJS(03) J3(14) J5(02) NMCC SECDEE(87) DPSECDEF
      NNIC SECDEF1 ASDI33A(10) 1DIA(15)
   •  SECSTATE WASH DC
   •  C I A
   •  NSA WASH DC
   •  WHITE HOUSE WASH DC
      CMC
   •  CSAF WASH DC
   •  CNO WASH DC
   •  CSA WASH DC
      FILE(1)
(053)


TRANSIT/230636Z/230810Z/001140TORR670664
DE RUOMHRA #9575 2670615
ZNY CCCCC
P 230636Z SEP 76
FM USDAO TEHRAN
TO RUEKJCS/DIA WASHDC
INFO RUEKJCS/SECDEF DEPSECDEF WASHDC
RUFRBAA/COMIDEASTFOR
RUDOECA/CINCUSAFE LINDSEY AS GE/INCF
RHFRAAB/CINCUSAFE RAMSTEIN AB GE/INOCN
RUSNAAA/EUDAC VAIHINGEN GER
RUSNAAA/USCINCEUR VAIHINGEN GER/ECJ-2
BT
                              1235 SEP76
THIS IS IR 6 846 0139 76
1. (U) IRAN
2. REPORTED UFO SIGHTING (U)
3. (U) NA
4. (U) 19 & 20 SEP 76
5. (U) TEHRAN, IRAN; 20 SEP 76
6. (U) F=6
7. (U) 6 846 0000 (NOTE RO COMMENTS)
8. (U) 6 846 0139 76
9. (U) R2SEP 76
10. (U) NA
11. (U) "INITIATE" IPSP PT-1440
PAGE  1                                        00110101  53
```

379/80-IR

098

A

Figure 7.2. The first page out of four of the "1976 Iran Incident" document.

The report mysteriously skips the part about what happened next. After the light was cast on the ground, did aliens come out? Was there an explosion? Did it fly away into the cosmos at light speed? We do not know.

The report changes topic and explains that the pilot regained communications and most of his controls and he began his return to the base. The pilot continued to have instrumentation problems along the way and, during his return back, saw a fourth UFO. When the pilot radioed this sighting to the tower, they reported again that no air traffic was in the area. So whatever this fourth object was, it too was unknown and should not have been in that vicinity.

The following morning, the second F-4 crew was flown by helicopter to the location where they believed the UFO may have landed the night before. Although they saw nothing on the ground, they questioned residents in a nearby house about the events that had recently unfolded. The residents reported seeing bright lights and hearing some loud noises, but that was all they reported. The last line of the report read that soil samples were taken for radiation testing, and the results would be forwarded when available.

That was the final line to this four-page document. Can you see why I was hooked? The story defies logic and contradicts all technology and aircraft that would become known in the decades after the event took place. It is my belief that we have yet to develop (that we know of) aircraft that can strategically shut off communications and shut down control panels, then instantly turn them back on when they no longer pose a threat, all while engaging in a dogfight. We also do not have many craft that can carry additional craft inside of them—very much like what a sci-fi novel would describe as a "mother ship." Yet this U.S. government document outlined all of that in the 1970s—and they never were able to solve the mystery.

One last thing I will point out about this record is what is called the "distribution list." Most intelligence reports begin with a list of who received that particular document. Just because a federal agency creates an intelligence report doesn't mean only that particular agency sees it or utilizes it for intelligence purposes. They will forward it to other agencies and federal departments that may benefit from the information.

The same is true with the DIA, and in this particular document, the "distribution list" was extensive. To name a few, this record was forwarded to the secretary of state, the Central Intelligence Agency (CIA), the National Security Agency (NSA), the Air Force, the Navy, and even to the president of the United States inside the White House.

Really digest those agencies I just named. Seven years after Project Blue Book closed, the DIA reported this UFO event to the military branch that

```
FEGEMMAYS00ILN118 
MULTY                                                    .99
ACTION
    DIAI
DISTR
    CJCS(01) DJS(03) J3(14) J5(02) NMCC SECDEE(07) OPSECDEF
    NMIC SECDEF1 ASD133A(10) 10IA(15)
•   SECSTATE WASH DC
•   C I A
•   NSA WASH DC
•   WHITE HOUSE WASH DC
    CMC
•   CSAF WASH DC
•   CNO WASH DC
•   CSA WASH DC
    FILE(1)
(053)
```

Figure 7.3.   The "distribution list" showing that the "1976 Iran Incident" document was sent to the White House.

claimed to have "solved" the UFO riddle; they sent it to other major intelligence agencies; and finally they found it necessary to brief the leader of the free world inside the White House. Each was kept apprised of this UFO intelligence, but why? There was no other value to the report, other than recording the UFO events of that night. So why did they all need to be kept in the loop about a topic that was already solved?

Using this document as a launching point, I began targeting the DIA with multiple FOIA requests. I figured if they had this one document, there had to be more. Instead of being specific and requesting exact case numbers, dates, places, and so forth, I requested the entire collection of "UFO documents" that they had in their possession.

I call this a "blanket request" wherein you ask for "all documents pertaining to . . . " vs. being specific and asking for "all documents pertaining to a UFO event in 1976 in Tehran, Iran." Although my first request to them was this specific, as I knew what I was requesting and trying to verify, this time I was asking for it all!

To my surprise, and after a few months of waiting, I received an answer. Well, kind of. The DIA sent me batches of UFO documents throughout multiple FOIA requests I had filed. Now, keep in mind that "company line" that is touted so much. No UFO-related document should exist after 1969, and although we proved that wrong with the 1976 Iran Incident document I outlined earlier, I was eager to see just how much additional information there was to find.

Surprisingly, the result was nearly 250 pages of material pertaining to UFOs. The dates of these documents were primarily *after* that 1969 cutoff date when there should not be anything, and it stretched well into the 1990s. Keep in mind that I requested this information in 1996 and 1997, so the fact that the responsive records were stretching into the 1990s proved to me, at this point, that the U.S. government and the intelligence agencies like the DIA were still keeping tabs on the UFO phenomenon and taking it very seriously.

Let me dissect some of the records to give you an idea on what this one agency has been hiding from you. The batch of records began with multiple reports throughout the Project Blue Book era. Although interesting, it mostly consisted of translated newspaper articles and brief "Intelligence Information Reports," or IIRs, profiling UFO encounters from Germany, New Zealand, Nepal, India, Uruguay, and many other countries throughout the world.

What is most interesting about many of these UFO cases is that they introduce a different project name associated with UFOs. This was not Project Blue Book, Project Sign, or Project Grudge, but rather, the DIA sent me declassified records from a project called Moon Dust.

Project Moon Dust was a research project that dealt with "unidentified objects," but the aim was slightly different than the UFO investigations by the Air Force that I have outlined thus far. Instead of investigating UFO reports of mysterious objects flying through the air, Project Moon Dust investigated unidentified objects that literally crashed to Earth.

The public explanation for Project Moon Dust is a bit less extraordinary than the thought that probably just went through your head. The objective did not necessarily mean it investigated alien craft that had crashed onto the surface of our planet, but rather, it was investigating the crashed debris that had fallen or broken off various space vehicles. It was the job of Project Moon Dust to figure out what they were, what country they came from, and what was the technology being utilized.

It is a bit unclear when Project Moon Dust actually began. Some researchers have argued Project Moon Dust began in the 1950s to investigate Soviet space technology that fell onto U.S. soil and into the hands of American scientists. However, these documents I received from the DIA show that Project Moon dust was investigating objects that fell back to Earth throughout the globe, not just the Soviet Union.

Of course, with an investigative objective like this, it has long been shrouded in secrecy and entwined into UFO conspiracy theories. Project Moon Dust is often cited as possibly being another covert operation that was responsible for taking in the most important UFO reports.

Was this the other "channel" that General Bolender mentioned in his memo, which dealt with cases that affected national security? Project Moon Dust documents are very hard to come by, as many seem to be either lost or destroyed. The question that remains to this day is: what exactly did Project Moon Dust discover?

This particular batch of DIA records does not answer that question, but it does deepen the UFO mystery. Following the chronology of the documents,

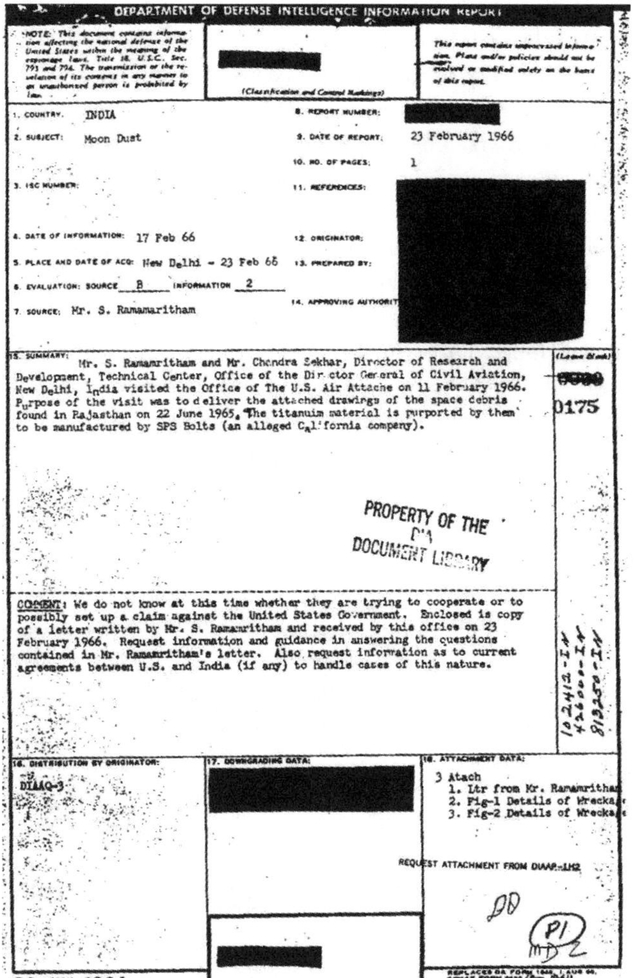

Figure 7.4.   A declassified page from the Project Moon Dust files, as released by the Defense Intelligence Agency (DIA).

you get to the 1969 cutoff date wherein the U.S. military and government alike denounced their UFO interest and yet the UFO intelligence gathered does not stop. This is a prime example of how the documents, yet again, contradict the "company line."

One specific "Intelligence Information Report" was dated August 22, 1974, more than four and a half years after Project Blue Book closed. Yet an unnamed intelligence officer (the name is redacted for privacy reasons) created a report of twenty-eight different UFO events that occurred in Spain, from the dates of September 1973 through June of 1974.

The witnesses that reported these cases consisted of school children, nurses, a chauffeur, a professor, newspaper photographers, an astronomy group, a teacher, and many others. The report showed the wide array of witnesses seeing the UFO phenomenon and described a plethora of sighting descriptions that went along with the reports.

One sighting recounted in this document, which occurred on March 23, 1974, was described as a "mother ship" which contained three other "ships" inside of it. The witness described the craft as a "Mother ship—aluminum, 150–200 meters long. Three smaller ships resembling mushrooms. Flew silently, had no windows by towers above and below." The document then stated that the witness "was pursued by one of the smaller ships, which disappeared as observer entered village of Castillo de las Guardas."

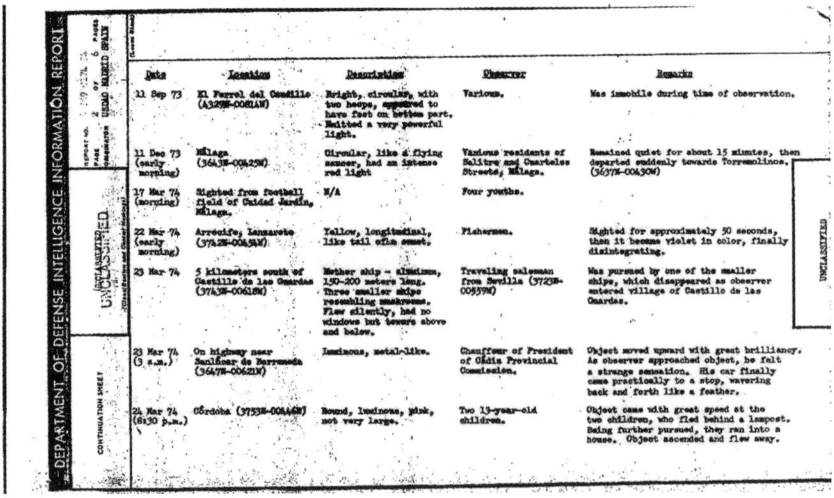
DEPARTMENT OF DEFENSE INTELLIGENCE INFORMATION REPORT

UNCLASSIFIED

CONTINUATION SHEET

Date	Location	Description	Observer	Remarks
11 Sep 73	El Ferrol del Caudillo (A329N-0081AW)	Bright, circular, with two hoops, appeared to have feet on bottom part. Emitted a very powerful light.	Various.	Was immobile during time of observation.
11 Dec 73 (early morning)	Málaga (3643N-00425W)	Circular, like a flying saucer, had an intense red light	Various residents of Salitre and Cuarteles Streets, Málaga.	Remained quiet for about 15 minutes, then departed suddenly towards Torremolinos. (3637N-00430W)
17 Mar 74 (morning)	Sighted from football field of Cuidad Jardín, Málaga.	N/A	Four youths.	
22 Mar 74 (early morning)	Arrecife, Lanzarote (3742N-00454W)	Yellow, longitudinal, like tail of a comet.	Fishermen.	Sighted for approximately 50 seconds, then it became violet in color, finally disintegrating.
23 Mar 74	5 kilometers south of Castillo de las Guardas (3743N-00618W)	Mother ship - aluminum, 150-200 meters long. Three smaller ships resembling mushrooms. Flew silently, had no windows but towers above and below.	Traveling salesman from Sevilla (3723N-00559W)	Was pursued by one of the smaller ships, which disappeared as observer entered village of Castillo de las Guardas.
23 Mar 74 (3 a.m.)	On highway near Sanlúcar de Barrameda (3647N-00621W)	Luminous, metal-like.	Chauffeur of President of Cádiz Provincial Commission.	Object moved upward with great brilliancy. As observer approached object, he felt a strange sensation. His car finally came practically to a stop, wavering back and forth like a feather.
24 Mar 74 (8:30 p.m.)	Córdoba (3753N-00446W)	Round, luminous, pink, not very large.	Two 13-year-old children.	Object came with great speed at the two children, who fled behind a lampost. Being further pursued, they ran into a house. Object ascended and flew away.

UNCLASSIFIED

Figure 7.5. This Intelligence Information Report, dated August 22, 1974, listed nearly thirty UFO reports.

This event occurred two years prior to the 1976 Iran Incident, and yet you have a nearly identical description. The witness in Spain described a craft that was able to "carry" multiple other UFOs inside of it, just like the military pilot witnessed in Iran. Yet, to this day, neither case has a viable explanation nor can we adequately explain the technology used.

Another report, dated April of 1978, reinforced the fact that not only was the phenomenon a global threat, but there were cases that continued to leave behind physical trace. This particular report, written by the U.S. Defense Attaché Office in Ottawa, Canada, detailed a sighting that happened near Bell Island, which is located off the Avalon Peninsula of Newfoundland and Labrador in Conception Bay.

The record details "streaks of super bright silvery white light." These streaks of light were connected to loud mysterious booms or explosions that were heard from Western Bay, which is on the North Shore of Conception Bay, all the way down as far south as Cape Broyale. This distance is more than one hundred kilometers and, with that fact, does make the theory of a "sonic boom" from conventional aircraft a bit less likely.

If that was not strange enough, the report ended explaining that this case is one of two events that happened in that region within a two-month time frame. The first event, six weeks prior to the incident outlined in this document, is said to have left impressions or holes in the ground approximately two feet in diameter and about two feet deep.

It should be noted, in the same paragraph, the unknown author of the message sent back to the DIA discounted the "flying saucer" theory, wherein it was written in the final lines of the document, "It is not precipitated by atomic explosions or flying saucers but may be catalyzed by high performance aircraft."

Although this theory posed at the end of the report seems plausible to explain the loud explosion-like noises, which absolutely could be attributed to a "sonic boom," it does not account for the holes and impressions left in the ground. You cannot solve these types of events by stating you have a fast-flying aircraft in the area that broke the sound barrier but then claim that somehow that same aircraft landed in the middle of its trek to explain the impressions left behind in the ground.

Other theories were touted, like a meteorite striking the Earth, which may account for the loud noise upon entry and potentially leaving the holes in the ground. However, this all ignores the fact that there are nearly identical reports of UFOs leaving impressions behind in the ground, like the one that occurred in Socorro, New Mexico, fourteen years prior in 1964.

The "distribution list" for this report also proved valuable. The CIA, secretary of state, NSA, and even the chief of staff of the U.S. Air Force, among others, all received this report as well. Yes, the head of the very agency that solved the UFO riddle was near the top of the list to hear about UFOs traversing the skies and leaving impressions in the dirt behind.

As the records entered the 1980s, a very new characteristic to UFO reports came to light: a dogfight between a UFO and a military aircraft. In a June 1980 message, sent from the U.S. Defense Attaché Office in Lima, Peru, a Peruvian Air Force officer reported that he along with a group of pilots were flying in formation, and they saw an unknown craft flying around them on multiple occasions.

First, they witnessed a UFO during the morning hours of May 9, 1980, and the second sighting was the next day, the evening of May 10, 1980. They described the object as round in shape, and it was hovering near the Mariano Melgar Air Base, La Joya, Peru. During the first encounter on May 9, the base commander scrambled an Su-22 aircraft to intercept the object.

The pilot of this aircraft, according to a "third party" as the report documents, did intercept the UFO and fire upon it—but there was absolutely no damage to the object that could be seen. The craft seemed to be indestructible. The Su-22 pilot then tried to loop around and do a second pass to intercept, but the UFO was too fast. It outran the Su-22 and got away.

The next evening, during the second encounter, another Su-22 was scrambled to intercept this UFO. Again, the UFO escaped, as its speed was simply too much for the engaging Su-22.

The Su-22 was a Soviet-made variant of what was called the Sukhoi Su-17—a variable-sweep wing fighter-bomber that was branded as the Su-22 and sold to many countries like Peru for use. It began testing in the late 1960, and was sold throughout the 1970s by the Soviet Union. It is believed that the Su-22 could reach speeds just more than Mach 1.5, or about 1,140 miles per hour, so although it was not the fastest aircraft in the sky, it could break the sound barrier and keep up in a chase. Well, most chases. These particular UFO encounters proved too much for the aircraft, and it just could not keep up.

The documented instance of firing upon a UFO is not the first within U.S. government files, but in the post–Blue Book era, it is the earliest I could find. It showed that the UFO phenomenon continued to be that threat to national security that they had denied, at the time this document was written, for more than a decade. And in case you are wondering, the chief of staff of the U.S. Air Force was yet again on the top of the list to hear about these UFO dogfights in Peru.

Toward the mid- to late 1980s, the DIA UFO documents took an odd turn to a tone of sarcasm. I really cannot tell you why this is, but despite this apparent lack of seriousness, the DIA continued to collect UFO intelligence from around the globe. What is not as easily discernible in these records is how serious the DIA was actually taking UFO reports at this point, since latter documents were written with such a sarcastic tone.

In fairness, that could have been part of a post–Project Blue Book tactic to discredit the topic and diminish any interest by the general public. The FOIA was on the books for more than a decade at the point that these documents were written, and it had enough time to be polished and utilized by the general public. So unlike the documents that were written in the early days of Project Grudge, Project Sign, and Project Blue Book, wherein they were written with no thought by the author that they would ever see the light of day, these documents were different. They were written by those that realized their intelligence, their writing, their opinions, their "facts," and their stories could absolutely be seen by the public if requested. So they had to be careful, and it's possible this was the introduction of sarcasm and humor embedded in the intelligence papers. That sarcasm would belittle the topic and decrease any aura of importance to the UFO cases they were collecting, while at the same time collecting the intelligence.

One example of this tone was written in 1987 by the Joint Chiefs of Staff. They wrote in a communication to the DIA dated October 1987, with the subject line, "UNIDENTIFIED FLYING OBJECTS OVER GHANA—II (U)," the following:

FOR WHATEVER REASON-PERHAPS EXTRA TERRESTRIAL INTERFERENCE REF MSG TRANSMISSION BECAME GARBLED. [[REDACTED]] [[REDACTED]] [[REDACTED]] IN THIS CASE, SPACE DEBRIS FROM WEATHER, COMMUNICATIONS, OR ONE OF THE COUNTLESS EXPERIMENTAL SATILLITES WHICH CIRCLE THE ATMOSPHERE APPEARS TO BE THE MOST PLAUSIBLE EXPLANATION. [[REDACTED]] [[REDACTED]] [[REDACTED]] [[REDACTED]] [[REDACTED]] [[REDACTED]] [[REDACTED]] WE HAVE NOTHING FURTHER, BUT UFOS ARE ALWAYS A TERRIFIC SUBJECT FOR COCKTAIL CHATTER AND MIGHT LEAD INTO OTHER SUBJECTS LIKE AIR DEFENSE AND SURVEILLANCE. HAPPY HALLOWEEN.

Another document that holds the same date and identical subject line, also written by the Joint Chiefs of Staff to the DIA, reads in paragraph 3:

UFOS REMAIN A CONCERN HERE, ALTHOUGH NOT HEAVILY PUBLICIZED, I THINK SOME WERE SUPPSED [sic] TO SHOW UP FOR THE

"HARMONICS CONVERGENCE" THIS SUMMER BUT ONLY INCAS COULD SEE THEM.) [[REDACTED]] [[REDACTED]] [[REDACTED]] [[REDACTED]] [[REDACTED]] [[REDACTED]] [[REDACTED]]

Although the sarcasm in some documents is palpable, the redacted information remains a big unanswered question. What won't they show us? The redacted portions of these records, which have no cited FOIA exemptions on

```
                                                          PAGE:0008
   INQUIRE=DOC3D
   ITEM NO=00918858
   ENVELOPE
   RTTCZYUW RUEKJCS3159 2970107-███████-RUEALGX.
   ZNY ████
   HEADER
   R 240107Z OCT 87
   FM JCS WASHINGTON DC
   INFO RUEALGX/SAFE
   R 231200Z OCT 87
   FM DIA WASHINGTON DC//DAH-6//
   ███████████
   BT
   CONTROLS

   ███ 15,412/DAH-6
   BODY
   SUBJ:  UNIDENTIFIED FLYING OBJECTS OVER GHANA (U)
   REF:  UR IIR███████████(201412Z AUG 87).
   1. ████ PRECISE IDENTIFICATION OF THE PHENOMENA DESCRIBED IN YOUR
   REPORT IS NOT PRESENTLY POSSIBLE.  HOWEVER, THE PATTERNS, ACCOMPANY-
   ING NOISE, AND COLORATIONS REPORTED STRONG SUGGEST SPACE DEBRIS FROM
   ATMOSPHERIC GRIDLOCK.

   3. ████ UFOS REMAIN A CONCERN HERE, ALTHOUGH NOT HEAVILY PUBLICIZED,
   I THINK SOME WERE SUPPSED TO SHOW UP FOR THE "HARMONICS CONVER-
   GENCE" THIS SUMMER BUT ONLY INCAS COULD SEE THEM.)

   PAGE 02 RUEKJCS3159███████████
   ADMIN
   ████████
   BT
   #3159



   NNNN
```

Figure 7.6. This Joint Chiefs of Staff record highlighted the sarcastic tone that soon invaded some UFO records.

why they are redacted, could help answer how serious these UFO cases were to the DIA and to the intelligence community as a whole.

In one letter, the DIA gave a blanket statement that the information withheld from me was due to FOIA exemptions (b)(1), (b)(2), and (b)(6)—which, respectively, translate to information that poses a threat to national security if released, the internal rules and practices of an agency, and finally information withheld because the release of that could be an unwarranted invasion of personal privacy. However, for decades, these records have never been properly broken down and redacted portions properly cited with which exemptions pertain to that information withheld.

This may seem brutally dry and nit-picking that I bring it up, but this is important for many reasons. More than anything else, it shows why a particular redacted line, paragraph, or page is being withheld. For example, information redacted because of (b)(1), which is national security information, is a lot different from withholding information under (b)(6), which is because it is a name, address, phone number, Social Security number, and so on. To be able to differentiate between the two (or technically between the nine exemptions in total) allows researchers like me to figure out how important that particular redaction is. Agencies are supposed to cite each blacked-out portion of their releases, but the DIA did not follow that rule.

And if you caught my reference to blacked-out "pages" above—you may want me to take that statement and prove it. Well, the DIA UFO records from the 1990s and beyond do just that.

To summarize the progression thus far, DIA UFO documents went from Project Blue Book–era intelligence, to clear threats to national security in the 1970s, to dogfights with indestructible UFOs in the early 1980s, and now, to some of the most heavily redacted UFO records you can find in the 1990s.

Strangely, many of the more interesting records, like that 1976 Iran Incident, the "UFO Dogfight" in 1980, and others, were considered "unclassified." That meant these intelligence records contained no classified information and could be released largely untouched if requested under the FOIA. Some exemptions like (b)(6) may still apply, so you may have minor redactions in an "unclassified" document, but it is released, and that is the case with some of the stories I have recounted here in this chapter. They are considered unclassified.

However, the 1990s-era records change that entirely. Beginning right in July of 1990, one document is nearly entirely blacked out and redacted and holds the subject line, "[[REDACTED]] UNIDENTIFIED LIGHTS (U)." There is one small section readable, which is paragraph 5 (paragraphs 1–4 were entirely blacked out), and it reads:

PAGE:0002

-    DEPARTMENT OF DEFENSE

DOI : (U) 900712.

REQS:

5. (U) JORDANIAN CIVILIANS HAVE REPORTED SEEING THE
LIGHTS FROM THE WESTERN SUBURBS OF AMMAN. ONE
REPORTED SEEING THE LIGHT "LATE IN THE EVENING" OF 11
JUL 90.

**Figure 7.7. This document highlights the heavily classi-
fied nature of some UFO documents that remain hidden
from the public.**

5. (U) JORDANIAN CIVILIANS HAVE REPORTED SEEING THE LIGHTS
FROM THE WESTERN SUBURBS OF AMMAN. ONE REPORTED SEE-
ING THE LIGHT "LATE IN THE EVENING" OF 11 JUL 90.

The classification designation itself is classified, meaning they blacked out
the entire designation and will not let you see if this record is "Top Secret,"
"Secret," "Confidential," and so on. Even with this record, I still find the "distribution list" of importance, not only because of who is on it but also the fact

that, compared to those from the 1970s, the list is getting larger. And yes, it still, even into the 1990s, includes the chief of staff of the U.S. Air Force.

I know some of my points are becoming repetitive, but they deserve repetition. It shows the absolute absurdity that the U.S. Air Force claims "no interest" in the UFO phenomenon, and yet intelligence agencies continue to brief them on UFO encounters for decades after their lie began.

Another document, also from June of 1990, was written by the Joint Chiefs of Staff, and it is also heavily redacted. However, in the portions you can read, it shows that possibly intelligence agencies were watching UFO research organizations around the globe.

It begins outlining a UFO seen in the Sichuan Province in March of 1990. The UFO measured about twenty meters long and flew silently. Then a sizable paragraph and nearly the entire following page of the record is fully redacted. Clearly, there is quite a bit of sensitive information, but then something becomes readable:

CHINA UNIDENTIFIED FLYING OBJECT (UFO) RESEARCH ORGA-NIZATION HOSTS NATIONAL CONFERENCE IN BEIJING ON 11 MAY (LAD, 14 MAY). THE ORGANIZATION HOPES THAT CHINA WILL BE SELECTED TO HOST THE FIRST WORLD UFO CONFER-ENCE, WHICH IS SCHEDULED FOR 1993. MORE THAN 200 CHINESE RESEARCHERS ARE ATTENDING THE CONFERENCE TO STUDY REPORTS OF FLYING SAUCERS OR "FEI DEI" (STC 7378/4308) IN CHINA. ABOUT 5,000 UFO SIGHTINGS HAVE BEEN REPORTED IN CHINA IN THE PAST 20 YEARS.

After this paragraph, another nearly entire page is classified and redacted. Does this prove that the DIA or a component of the Department of Defense (DOD)/Joint Chiefs of Staff was watching UFO research organizations worldwide? What is so secretive and classified about anything related to this? One could argue that a reference like the paragraph above is simply just documenting the event in China. Yet the information is sandwiched between pages of redacted and classified information.

It seems like the more recent the document, the more classified it is. As the years ticked on throughout the 1990s, more UFO intelligence was received and collected by the DIA, and the later documents held "Secret" and even "Top Secret" designations, proving that the information on those records was more sensitive than in the decades prior.

These stacks of papers I received from the DIA tell an amazing story. I have only outlined a select few from the decades covered by this document release, but they alone can prove beyond a doubt that the UFO phenomenon is very real and is absolutely a threat. In addition, the "distribution lists" confirm that the upper echelons of the U.S. intelligence community, and even those close to whoever sat in the Oval Office, were all kept very much in the loop about these UFO events.

Although the UFO phenomenon was proving to be a global problem, the records did not just deal with off-shore encounters. Rather, in another request I sent to the Office of the Assistant Secretary of Defense (OASD), which is under the DOD, I received a new batch of material that began to show me this phenomenon may become more *dangerous* than it has been *interesting*.

UFOS INVADE
THE U.S. MILITARY

The Defense Intelligence Agency (DIA) records showed me that the UFO phenomenon was nothing unique to America. Around the globe, whatever these UFOs were, they were showing they were not always "friendly." From UFOs strategically shutting down jet aircraft to in some cases crashing on Earth and being collected under a "SECRET" military project, the UFO phenomenon was becoming a dangerous one to go unchallenged.

In another batch of FOIA records that I received, this time from the Office of the Assistant Secretary of Defense (OASD), I was able to sift through documents that pertained specifically to America. Although the global reports from the DIA were fascinating to look at, for me to see the records that dealt with cases in my own backyard, now that was what I really seeking more than anything else.

The OASD records began with a short seven-page summary of Project Blue Book. I had never seen this particular record before and found it rather strange because, having been written in 1966, it actually got a lot wrong about the program it was chronicling. For example, there was this strange paragraph:

> The Air Force has no films, photographs, maps, charts, or graphs of unidentified flying objects. Photographs that have been submitted for evaluation in conjunction with UFO reports have been determined to be a misinterpretation of natural or conventional objects. These objects have a positive identification.

This is another example of a statement that was not entirely true. The "explanations" that Project Blue Book put forth on many photographs and film reels submitted to them were questionable at best. Here in 1966, this particular document was giving the impression that everything was solved, when we can actually prove otherwise. It further gives evidence that the real story behind the scenes was actually wildly different than the story given to the press and the public.

Of course, at the top of the stack, was the familiar "UFO Fact Sheet" that seemed to be coming at me from nearly every office I filed FOIA requests to. It held the same "facts" as previous versions I received and have already gone over, but humorously, the records that came after the "fact sheets" (as this packet of material contained multiple versions of it) contradict nearly every "fact" on it. It is like they were hiding the evidence to prove a cover-up in plain sight. The first pages claim there was nothing to the UFO topic, followed by UFO documents that proved the contrary. It does not get much more blatant than that.

For example, right under the fact sheet telling us all that UFOs do not pose a national security threat was a memorandum from the National Military Command Center (NMCC) in 1975 with the subject of "AFB Penetration." This document states:

1. At 290200 EST AFOC informed NMCC that an unidentified helicopter, possibly two, had been sighted flying low over Loring AFB Maine, in proximity to a weapons storage area.
2. An Army National Guard helo was called in to assist in locating the unidentified helo(s).
3. NORAD was informed of the incident by SAC, requested and received authority from Canadian officials to proceed into Canadian airspace if necessary to locate the intruder.
4. At 0404 SAC Command Center informed NMCC that the army helo assisting on the scene had not sighted the unidentified helo(s).
5. A similar incident was reported at Loring the evening of 28 October 1975.

Here is what is very interesting about this document. It was written about five years after the official close of Project Blue Book but is the first instance of what appeared to be a sleight of hand by the U.S. military. Do not call a spade a spade but rather think of another term that says the same thing but does not have the same effect as "UFO"; in this case, "unidentified helicopter" or "unidentified helo."

What confuses me a bit is the fact that it is a bit of an oxymoron to call it an "unidentified helicopter" because you're calling it a helicopter; therefore, to a point, it is identified. Maybe I am reading into that part too much, but it reads to me like they were attempting to characterize a UFO as something that it was not. Regardless of what they really meant, it is a UFO, it was encroaching on the weapons storage area of Loring Air Force Base, and it was a threat.

N M C C
THE NATIONAL MILITARY COMMAND CENTER
WASHINGTON, D.C. 20301

29 October 1975
0605 EST

MEMORANDUM FOR RECORD

Subject: AFB Penetration

1. At 290200 EST AFOC informed NMCC that an unidentified helicopter, possibly two, had been sighted flying low over Loring AFB Maine, in proximity to a weapons storage area.

2. An Army National Guard helo was called in to assist in locating the unidentified helo(s).

3. NORAD was informed of the incident by SAC, requested and recieved authority from Canadian officials to proceed into Canadian airspace if necessary to locate the intruder.

4. At 0404 SAC Command Center informed NMCC that the army helo assisting on the scene had not sighted the unidentified helo(s).

5. A similar incident was reported at Loring the evening of 28 October 1975.

C. D. ROBERTS, JR.
Brigadier General, USMC
Deputy Director for
Operations (NMCC)

Distribution:
CJCS (5)	CSA	PA REP
DJS (3)	CNO	WEST HEM DESK
J-30	CSAF	NWSB
J-31	CMC	NMCC BRIEFER
J-32	CH, WWMCCS OPS & EVAL DIV	
J-32A	DDO (NMCC)	
J-33	ADDO (NMCC)	
J-34	CCOC (NMCC)	
J-35	DIA REP FOR NMIC	
J-38	NSA REP	
	CIA REP	

Figure 8.1. National Military Command Center (NMCC) memorandum describing the penetration of airspace by UFOs, referred to as "unidentified helos," over Loring Air Force Base, Maine, in 1975.

Worthy of note for this particular document as well: the "distribution list." These get rather boring, I know, but they are crucial to understanding exactly where documents are sent and whom they are distributed to in order to keep them apprised of UFO occurrences. This particular report's "distribution list" included the chief of staff of the U.S. Air Force (CSAF), the Chief of Naval Operations

(CNO), the DIA, the National Security Agency (NSA), and the Central Intelligence Agency (CIA) among others.

This is yet more proof that there was no stopping the interest in UFOs; it was a top priority to our intelligence agencies and the phenomenon was indeed a threat. The next few pages of the stack dealt with this specific incident, and each record began offering additional details that the previous one had not.

One page recounting the Loring AFB incursions referenced the Army National Guard having scrambled an attack helicopter to engage the UFO. It stated:

> At approximately 290100 EST Oct 75, one unidentified helicopter was sighted at an altitude of 150 feet at approximately 200 to 500 meters from a weapons storage area at Loring AFB, ME. At 290300 EST Oct 75, the unidentified helicopter was sighted over the weapons storage area. In both instances, an Army National Guard (NG) helicopter responded, but was unable to contact or identify the intruder. MG Sniffin, DA Director of Ops, DCSOPS, approved the following procedures for any similar incident effective until 300800 EST Oct 75:
>
> - NG helicopter and crew placed in "full time training duty" (FTTD).
> - NG helicopter may enter Canadian airspace with consent of Canadian authorities.
> - NG helicopter employment limited to tracking and identification.
> - Only U.S. military personnel and if considered necessary representatives from the FBI, FAA, and Border Patrol will be embarked in the NG helicopter.

This seems rather exciting for a phenomenon that does not exist. The National Guard was engaging the object, to no avail, and possibly these engagements would include representatives from the Federal Bureau of Investigation (FBI), the Federal Aviation Administration (FAA), and Border Patrol. This was a multi-agency effort to engage the threat, and yet again, they were unable to identify or even find their target. That is some "unidentified helicopter"!

These documents also show that this was not one encroachment at Loring AFB but actually many. Another record explains that another aircraft entered the hunt. This particular document is very hard to read (which is oddly the norm of documents that have an interesting story to tell), but here are some excerpts that can be read:

> A sighting was made of a helicopter in the same general location as the sighting last night.

OPREP-3 Pinnacle JJ0033, Visual contact was made [unreadable] meters from the weapons storage area at an altitude of 157ft. At [unreadable] Air Guard helicopter 359712 was launched by made negative visual contact.

The helicopter was visually sighted by SCS at 290800Z over the weapons storage area. The local guard helicopter was airborn [sic] at [unreadable] but again made no contact.

The unknown aircraft did not display lighting. Ground personnel were able to direct the Air Guard helicopter to within 1000ft of the unknown aircraft, with both helicopters in sight, but visual acquisition was not made. During this period a KC-135 was orbiting at 5000ft [unreadable] to aid in identification and to act as rapid relat. At [unreadable] all contact was lost. It is our opinion that the unknown helicopter has demonstrated a clear intent in the weapons storage area, is smart and a most capable aviator.

Local security has been increased. We anticipate further incidents accordingly. We will request the continued presence of Air Guard helicopters.

We plan to pursue into Canada if necessary.

We have coordinated with Maine State Police and the Royal Canadian Mounted Police and have been assured of the complete cooperation of both.

R.C.M.P. will respond to any landing site in Canadian territory.

Local security police aboard Air Guard helicopter have been ordered to use discretion and await R.C.M.P. arrival for any apprehension in Canadian territory.

This seemed like war. Encroachments on a weapons storage area, which may actually cross country lines into Canada, all seem like acts of aggression. These particular incidents alone outline exactly why a UFO research program should be under way and should have never ended in 1969/1970 with the close of Project Blue Book. Alien or not, these UFOs, or "unidentified helicopters" if you want to call them that, displayed clear intelligence and an agenda to invade sensitive airspace.

In case you're wondering, the "distribution list" on this particular document included all the players we have already mentioned but now included another one absent from some previous reports about the Loring AFB incursions: the White House. The president of the United States, at this time being President Gerald Ford, was kept apprised of these UFOs encroaching into sensitive weapon storage areas.

The next month, in November of 1975, the UFOs returned to the location nearby Loring AFB. One document, only dated "Nov 75," states:

At 312317 EST, a visual sighting of an unidentified object was reported 4 nautical miles northwest of Loring AFB, Maine. The alert help at Loring was launched to identify the object but was unable to make contact. The alert helo was launched again at 010146 EST in response to a slow moving target picked up by RAP-CON. This [unreadable] was also unable to make contact with the object.

This particular document reinforces one fact about these UFOs that encroached into Loring AFB in 1975. It talks about this "unidentified object"

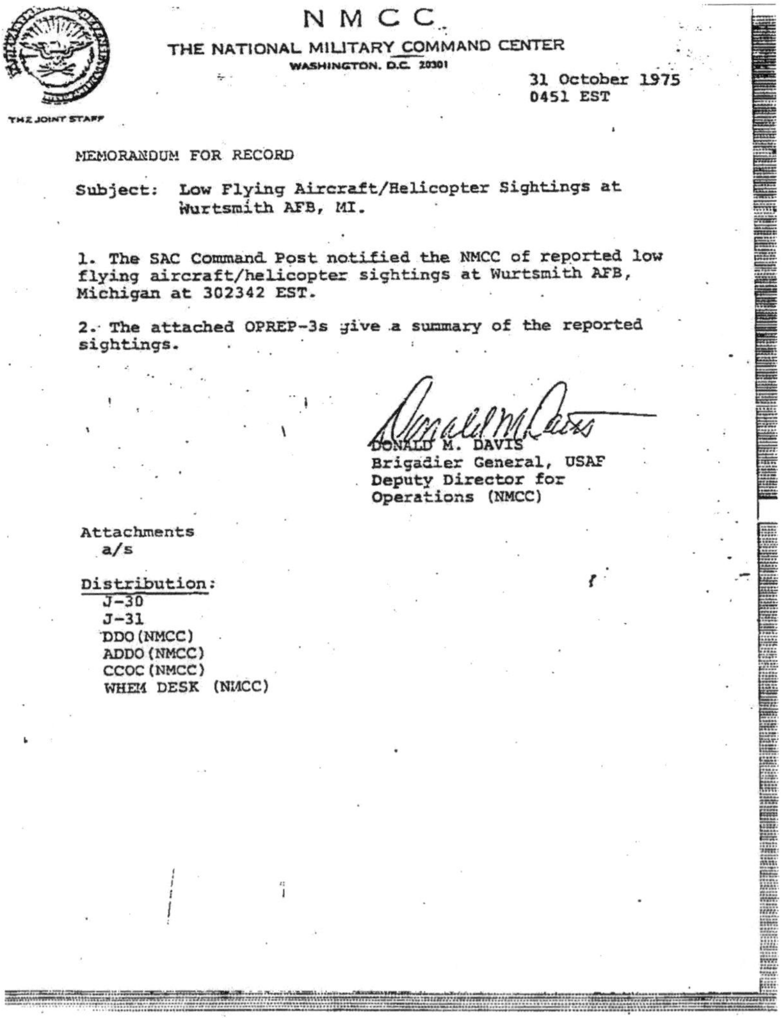

Figure 8.2. National Military Command Center (NMCC) memorandum regarding the UFOs, referred to as "low flying aircraft/helicopter sightings," in 1975.

being "slow moving," yet not a single National Guard aircraft could find it or catch it. How is that even possible?

Beginning the same month as the Loring AFB sightings, Wurtsmith Air Force Base in Michigan also got hit with multiple sightings. A memorandum dated October 31, 1975, also from the NMCC, states:

Subject: Low Flying Aircraft/Helicopter Sightings at Wurtsmith AFB, MI.

1. The SAC Command Post notified the NMCC of reported low flying aircraft/ helicopter sightings at Wurtsmith AFB, Michigan at 302342 ETS.
2. The attached OPREP-3s give a summary of the reported sightings.

The attached report reads:

SAC (Lt. Col. Giordano) reports that an unidentified helicopter with no lights came up over the back gate of Wurtsmith and hovered over the Weapons Storage Area and then moved on. RAPCON had it painted for a short period. A tanker at 2700 feet had visual and skin paint out over Lake Huron for about 20 miles heading SE. Tanker reports he thinks he saw a second skin paint. The tanker lost all contact about 35 miles SE of the base over the lake. Tanker is still flying trying to locate by means of telephonic search with FAA and RAPCON. Increased security initiated at Wurtsmith.

31/0030E Update: Lt Col Giordano (SAC Senior Controller) updates and corrects the above information as follows: An unidentified low flying aircraft came up over the backgate of Wurtsmith and was visually sighted in the vicinity of the motor pool. RAPCON showed several aircraft at the time, one near the WSA (there was no hovering as previously reported). A tanker was dispatched and had visual and skin paint out over Lake Huron of a low flying aircraft (with lights on) heading SE at approximately 150 knots.

Tanker reports that the aircraft appeared to be joined by another aircraft (with its lights on also). Tanker reports that both aircraft then turned out their lights simultaneously, as if on signal. Tanker lost all contact approximately 35 NM SE of the base. Upon information that the Dept of Natural Resources sends out aircraft searching for hunters spotting deer, the Dept of Natural Resources was contacted; however, they maintain none of their aircraft were in the area at the time.

The sightings then continued at Malmstrom Air Force Base, in Montana. Beginning in November of 1975, one particular document recounts the events:

From 080253 EST Nov 75 to 080420 EST Nov 75, Malmstrom AFB MT and four SAC sites reported a series of visual and radar contacts with unidentified flying objects. Several reports from the same locations included jet engine sounds associated with the observed bright lights. Two interceptors scrambled from the 24th NORAD Region failed to make contact with the UFO's.

The UFO sightings occurred on an extremely clear night. Visibility was 45 miles. Although northern lights will cause phenomena similar to the received reports, weather services indicated no possibility of the northern lights during the period in question. (SOURCE: NMCC MFR 080600 EST NOV 75.)

This document further reveals that this phenomenon was captured not only by the human eye but on radar. Normally, if events such as these were to occur only on one Air Force base at a given time, it is possible that a group of hostiles were attempting to access a weapons storage depot but obviously targeting one particular base. With this batch of records, we can confirm that in October and November of 1975, the U.S. military documented multiple UFO encounters throughout multiple Air Force bases, in which they could not neutralize the threat.

I have written it once, but I will write it again because it deserves repeating. These cases are a prime example of why a UFO research program is needed to this day and should never have stopped. Time and time again records were confirming the UFO phenomenon is not only real, but it is a threat the military has trouble accurately identifying and even warding off when it encroaches on sensitive airspace.

Despite the need for such a program, that did not stop the U.S. military trying to debunk the issue. On one hand, they were thoroughly documenting these UFO encounters, flying at such speeds that humans had not yet achieved; but on the other hand, they were attempting to lock down an explanation for these events.

In a message "Deputy Director of Operations [DDO] Update" dated November 13, 1975, it was requested:

In future UFO sightings, the WEST HEM Desk Officer will initiate telephone requests to the Senior Duty Officer at the Air Force Global Weather Central (AF-GWC) for a temperature inversion analysis in the vicinity of unusual sightings. The telephone response by AFGWC will be followed with a priority message.

In a document dated the same day, November 13, 1975, the NMCC issued a memorandum regarding "temperature inversion analysis," and they document a meeting with a representative from the AFGWC. It appeared that they were pushing hard and fast to get the whole temperature inversion analyses fast tracked in order to "explain" UFOs. The record stated:

MEMORANDUM FOR RECORD
Subject: Requests for Temperature Inversion Analysis

1. LTC Schmidt, representing Air Force Global Weather Central (AFGWC), visited the NMCC at 131500 EST to discuss arrangements to implement the procurement of weather information desired by CJCS, which is the subject of DDO Environmental Services memo of 13 November 1975. The following agreements with LTC Schmidt were reached:
   a. The West Hem Desk Officer will act as the control officer for temperature inversion analysis requests initiated by the NMCC. These requests will be made in conjunction with sightings of unusual phenomenon along the northern US border.
   b. Each telephone request will be serialized, i.e., (TIA #1 etc.) and directed to the duty officer at AFGWC, autovon 866-1661 or 271-2586. AFGWC will provide the requested analyses by telephone followed up by a priority message.
   c. A record of the serialized requests/responses will be maintained by the West Hem Desk Officer.

C. D. Roberts, Jr.
Brigadier General, USMC
Deputy Director for Operations, NMCC

I know what you're thinking—what in the world is "temperature inversion analysis" and how does that pertain to UFOs? Well, during the Project Blue Book era, an explanation was devised that attempted to explain some UFO sightings as being caused by a "temperature inversion." This is where a layer of warm air is trapped under a layer of cold air, thus potentially causing a mirage of some sort on radar or to the human eye. It is believed in these circumstances, the mirage is caused by a distant light on the group, which could then be reflected in the sky within this "temperature inversion."

Yeah, I laughed as well. So do not worry if that all sounds like a sad attempt at explaining UFO sightings because I agree with you. However, these declassified records showed that after these military base encounters, the NMCC decided to push forward toward explaining them all, or at least in part, as these "temperature inversions."

There was a huge problem continuing to brew that thwarted this effort to explain away the phenomenon. UFO encounters on sensitive military installations continued and went well beyond the October and November 1975 events. For example, another NMCC declassified document outlined a UFO encounter at Cannon Air Force Base in New Mexico. The memorandum was dated January 21, 1976, and outlined the incident:

> Two UFOs are reported near the flight line at Cannon AFB, New Mexico. Security Police observing them reported the UFOs to be 25 yards in diameter, gold or silver in color with blue light on top, hole in the middle and red light on bottom. Air Force is checking with radar. Additionally, checking weather inversion data.

(Signature)
J.B. MORIN
Rear Admiral, USN
Deputy Director for Operations, NMCC

There it was, "checking weather inversion data" in the last line, seemingly attempting to show that "weather inversions" were going to play a role in every UFO investigation—but highly unlikely a twenty-five-yard diameter object with a blue light and hole in the middle seen by multiple security officers could be explained as such.

Ten days after this incident, another NMCC memorandum was written dated January 31, 1976. This time, a UFO was sighted near Eglin Air Force Base, Florida. This document read the following:

MEMORANDUM FOR RECORD
Subject: Unidentified Flying Object Sighting

1. At 310805 received phoncon from AFOC: MG Lane, CG, Armanent and Development Test Center, Eglin AFB, Florida called and reported a UFO sighting from 0430 EST to 0600 EST. Security Policemen spotted lights from what they called a UFO near an Elgin radar site.
2. Photographs of the lights were taken. The Eglin Office of Information has made a press release on the UFO.
3. The temperature inversion analysis indicated no significant temperature inversion at Eglin AFB at the time. The only inversion present was due to radiation from the surface to 2500 feet. The Eglin surface conditions were clear skies, visibility 10–14 miles, calm winds, shallow ground fog on the runway, and a surface temperature of 44 degree F.

(Signature)
FRED A. TREYZ
Brigadier General, USAF
Deputy Director for
Operations (NMCC)

This document re-introduced that problem that I said earlier was brewing, that was thwarting the effort to explain UFO sightings as temperature inversions. Now, as these declassified records showed, they could not do it. Scientific data proved beyond a doubt that there were no temperature or weather inversions at the time of these UFO events, and these documents prove that attempt at an explanation fell apart. The military was back to square one. They had a UFO problem with no explanation.

The military base invasions continued, with this July 30, 1976, NMCC memorandum. In this document, it is said:

Subject: Reports of Unidentified Flying Object (UFOs)

1. At approximately 0345 EDT, the ANMCC called to indicate they had received several reports of UFO's in the vicinity of Fort Richie. The following events summarize the reports (times are approximate).
   a. 0130—Civilians reported a UFO sighting near Mt. Airy Md. This information was obtained via a call from the National Aeronautics Board (?) to Fort Richie Military Police.
   b. 0255—Two separate patrols from Site R reported sighting 3 oblong objects with a reddish tint, moving east to west. Personnel were located at separate locations on top of the mountain at Site R.
   c. 0300—Desk Sgt at Site R went to the top of the Site R mountain and observed a UFO over the ammo storage area at 100-200 yards altitude.
   d. 0345—An Army Police Sgt on the way to work at Site R reported sighting a UFO in the vicinity of Site R.
2. ANMCC was requested to have each individual write a statement on the sightings. One individual stated the object was about the size of a 2 1/2 ton truck.
3. Based on a JCS memorandum, subject: Temperature Inversion Analysis, dated 13 November 1975, the NMCC contacted the Air Force Global Weather Central. The Duty Officer, LTC OVERBY, reported that the Dulles International Airport observations showed two temperature inversions existed at the time of the alleged sightings. The first extended from the surface to 1,000 feet absolute and the second existed between 27,000 and 30,000 feet, absolute. He also said the atmosphere between 12,000 and 20,000 feet was heavily saturated with moisture. A hard copy message will follow.

(Signature)
L.J LEBLANC, Jr
Brigadier General, USMC
Deputy Director for
Operations, NMCC

This particular document actually was able to find evidence of a "temperature inversion" at the time of the sighting. I will let you all reading this decide if you feel that such a weather anomaly could account for multiple witnesses seeing three oblong objects moving east to west from various locations. If you are like me, you will not quite buy that explanation and will believe that this probably was, like so many documents that came before this one, a sighting of physical craft over a weapons storage area.

What is also something worthy of note is the precise location of the sighting. "Site R" is also known as the Raven Rock Mountain Complex. It is a U.S. military installation, complete with an underground nuclear bunker known as the "Underground Pentagon." This bunker is equipped with emergency operation centers for the U.S. Army, Navy, and Air Force and is believed to have been the location that Vice President Dick Cheney was taken to after the terrorist attacks on September 11, 2001.

There are multiple underground facilities throughout the nation that are used to house the president, vice president, members of Congress, and others in order to maintain "continuity of government." Back in 2000, I requested documents on "Site R" from the Department of Defense (DOD) and was surprised to have actually received cutaway diagrams of the facility.

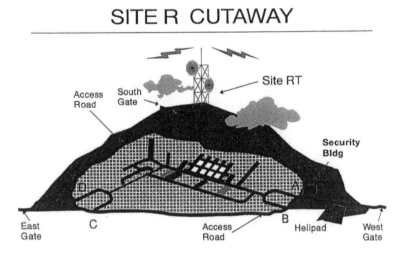

Figure 8.3. Declassified cutaway diagram of the "Site R" location, as released by the Department of Defense (DOD).

FACILITY LAYOUT

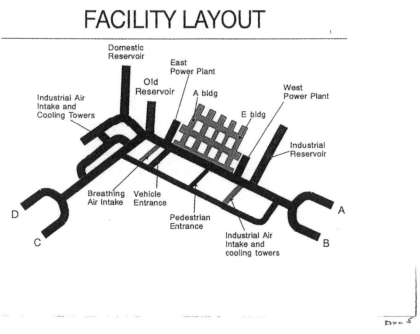

Figure 8.4. Declassified cutaway diagram of the "Site R" facility layout, as released by the Department of Defense (DOD).

Regardless of this facility's existence being acknowledged by the U.S. government (as many locations of the underground facilities are classified), security is incredibly tight. These bunkers are heavily guarded around the clock, to ensure that when they are needed, they are prepared and secure for the arrival of whoever may require it. Yet, in this particular case as well, the security and precautions that "Site R" undertook was no match for the three UFOs seen by multiple witnesses in 1976. Was it all just a weather inversion? Highly unlikely.

Declassified documents reveal that, not long after these UFO encounters took place in the mid- to late 1970s, another UFO case occurred on December 27, 1980, in Rendlesham Forest, Suffolk, England, outside the military base known as RAF Woodbridge. At the time, this base was utilized by the U.S. Air Force, as granted to them by the United Kingdom's Air Ministry, starting in 1952. In this January 13, 1981, declassified document, with Department of the Air Force letterhead, Col. Charles Halt summarizes the case:

1. Early in the morning of 27 Dec 80 (approximately 0300L), two USAF
   security police patrolmen saw unusual lights outside the back gate at RAF

Woodbridge. Thinking an aircraft might have crashed or been forced down, they called for permission to go outside the gate to investigate. The on-duty flight chief responded and allowed three patrolmen to proceed on foot. The individuals reported seeing a strange glowing object in the forest. The object was described as being metallic in appearance and triangular in shape, approximately two to three meters across the base and approximately two meters high. It illuminated the entire forest with a white light. The object itself had a pulsing red light on top and a bank(s) of blue lights underneath. The object was hovering or on legs. As the patrolmen approached the object, it maneu-

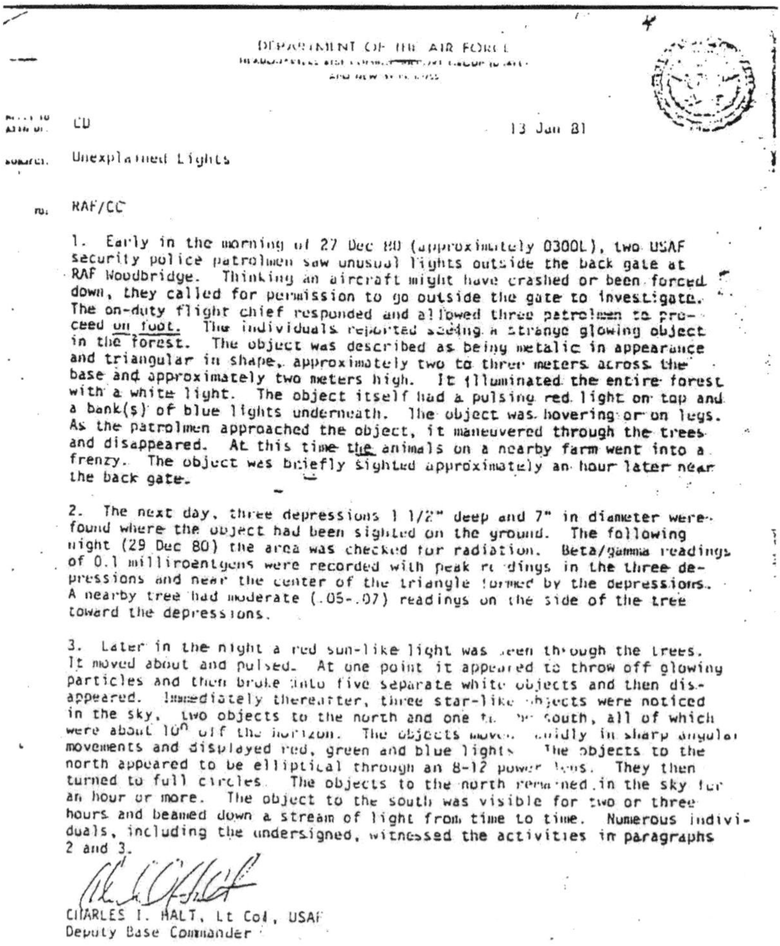

DEPARTMENT OF THE AIR FORCE

13 Jan 81

Unexplained Lights

RAF/CC

1. Early in the morning of 27 Dec 80 (approximately 0300L), two USAF security police patrolmen saw unusual lights outside the back gate at RAF Woodbridge. Thinking an aircraft might have crashed or been forced down, they called for permission to go outside the gate to investigate. The on-duty flight chief responded and allowed three patrolmen to proceed on foot. The individuals reported seeing a strange glowing object in the forest. The object was described as being metalic in appearance and triangular in shape, approximately two to three meters across the base and approximately two meters high. It illuminated the entire forest with a white light. The object itself had a pulsing red light on top and a bank(s) of blue lights underneath. The object was hovering or on legs. As the patrolmen approached the object, it maneuvered through the trees and disappeared. At this time the animals on a nearby farm went into a frenzy. The object was briefly sighted approximately an hour later near the back gate.

2. The next day, three depressions 1 1/2" deep and 7" in diameter were found where the object had been sighted on the ground. The following night (29 Dec 80) the area was checked for radiation. Beta/gamma readings of 0.1 milliroentgens were recorded with peak readings in the three depressions and near the center of the triangle formed by the depressions. A nearby tree had moderate (.05-.07) readings on the side of the tree toward the depressions.

3. Later in the night a red sun-like light was seen through the trees. It moved about and pulsed. At one point it appeared to throw off glowing particles and then broke into five separate white objects and then disappeared. Immediately thereafter, three star-like objects were noticed in the sky, two objects to the north and one to the south, all of which were about 10° off the horizon. The objects moved rapidly in sharp angular movements and displayed red, green and blue lights. The objects to the north appeared to be elliptical through an 8-12 power lens. They then turned to full circles. The objects to the north remained in the sky for an hour or more. The object to the south was visible for two or three hours and beamed down a stream of light from time to time. Numerous individuals, including the undersigned, witnessed the activities in paragraphs 2 and 3.

CHARLES I. HALT, Lt Col, USAF
Deputy Base Commander

Figure 8.5. Memorandum, written by Lt. Col. Charles Halt, recounting the Rendlesham Forest UFO encounter.

vered through the trees and disappeared. At this time the animals on a nearby farm went into a frenzy. The object was briefly sighted approximately an hour later near the back gate.

2. The next day, three depressions 1 1/2" deep and 7" in diameter were found where the object had been sighted on the ground. The following night (29 Dec 80) the area was checked for radiation. Beta/gamma readings of 0.1 milliroentgens were recorded with peak readings in the three depressions and near the center of the triangle formed by the depressions. A nearby tree had moderate (.05–.07) readings on the side of the tree toward the depressions.

3. Later in the night a red sun-like light was seen through the trees. It moved about and pulsed. At one point it appeared to throw off glowing particles and then broke into five separate white objects and then disappeared. Immediately thereafter, three star-like objects were noticed in the sky, two objects to the north and one to the south, all of which were about 10 degrees off the horizon. The objects moved rapidly in sharp angular movements and displayed red, green and blue lights. The objects to the north appeared to be elliptical through an 8–12 power lens. They then turned to full circles. The objects to the north remained in the sky for an hour or more. The object to the south was visible for two or three hours and beamed down a stream of light from time to time. Numerous individuals, including the undersigned, witnessed the activities in paragraphs 2 and 3.

Charles I. Halt, Lt. Col. USAF
Deputy Base Commander

This particular case is very controversial, as many witnesses have come forward to recount varying degrees of details related to the case. However, I reproduced the "Halt Memo" above to show that despite the varying versions of the story that have surfaced since the event in 1981, this official record, authored by the same agency that claims there is nothing to the UFO phenomenon, displays something quite extraordinary.

Whenever physical effects are left behind—like in this particular case, multiple impressions in the ground—it confirms that something physical was involved. Many skeptics may attempt to dismiss such UFO encounters as misidentified aircraft or even hallucinations, but no viable explanation has ever surfaced to explain this encounter, nor the many others that have surfaced in the post–Project Blue Book era.

Beyond analyzing these documents from the 1970s and 1980s, I further aimed to prove that the UFO phenomenon was a threat, not that more evidence was needed. I filed a FOIA request to Space Command, headquartered at Peterson

Air Force Base, first in February of 1997. I sought all UFO documentation and waited for a response.

In July of that same year, I was sent an envelope from Space Command. To my surprise, a single-page log file of various UFO reports, spanning from February of 1995 through July of 1996, was released. Given the fact that my request was in 1997, and there were numerous reports collected by Space Command in just only about a year prior, it showed me that the UFO phenomenon was still very active and still creating a nuisance. The document broke down various UFO encounters:

Summary of Unusual Sightings

16 Feb 95 1920Z Received a call about a fireball SE of Denver and E of Colo Spgs. Report by phone at 041 S am from Denver.

16 Jun 95 2107 MDT 31st Avenue, Calgary, Alberta, Canada. Couple saw bright descent light near Bull River Dam at high speed, then faded to two second duration, traveling west.

19 Jun 95 0501Z Received by phone. Single bright circling light in SW Calgary, Alberta, Canada.

19 Jun 95 0540Z Calgary, Alberta, bright light flying east, orange to red to purple, huge and silent 2-3 second duration.

30 Jul 95 0420Z Reported UFO sighting in Victoria BC. Bright white light hovered above a house for several minutes.

31 Jul 95 0736 New York. Red and blue light in the sky. The star appeared to break into two stars. No correlation found.

16 May 96 08002 Received call of UFO sighting at Griffiss AFB NY. Four enlisted men observed circular orange light just above tree line ESE of their location. Five minutes total hovered and then disappeared. Reported via CONRINEADS.

22 Jun 96 0515Z Received call of falling star which exploded in Eastern Colorado.

14 Jul 96 Six people saw rotating object with three lights in Missasauga, Ontario, Canada time.

15 Jul 96 0230Z. Weather clear, no noise, observed one mile away for 30 seconds, then object reversed direction and disappeared over horizon.

Although they condensed it into a single typed page, the logs came from various handwritten notebooks at the facility. As a courtesy, they combined them all into a single page, along with giving me copies of the original handwritten logs for reference. Once I saw those, I was thankful for the typed translation because the handwriting was incredibly difficult to read.

There are two particular key points with the release of these log files. First is the fact that Space Command, headquartered at an Air Force Base, would collect UFO sighting reports at all. That contradicted the "company line" and went against what the Air Force was preaching about the topic. However, second, in the logs was another encounter at a U.S. military installation, namely Griffiss Air Force Base in New York. The witnesses included four enlisted airmen, who all saw a UFO and reported it. Again, this contradicted that "company line" they have been touting for decades, but it also began a long list of clues, which you will see in the next few chapters, that would allow me to make an amazing discovery.

Although these documents are all crucial to proving the cover-up, they are only the tip of the iceberg when it comes to dissecting how deep the conspiracy goes.

THE NUCLEAR
CONNECTION

Continuing the thread of the "national security threat," you just read through multiple encounters on or around sensitive military installations; some, like Loring Air Force Base, held nuclear arsenals. Not only is it common sense that you just are not able to fly your crop-dusting helicopters into military airspace, there are laws prohibiting such actions. So, as declassified documents clearly show within a decade of the close to Project Blue Book, there was ample evidence that this was an ongoing issue with no explanation and it needed to be dealt with.

Incidents like the ones you just read in the previous chapter make us question whether or not UFOs are drawn to nuclear weapons or nuclear technology. However, to strengthen the concept of this "national security threat" even more—not that you need it—declassified records also show that there has been a long history to UFO incursions on or around sensitive nuclear storage facilities. These cases stretched all the way back to the beginning days of UFO research by the U.S. military. One FBI memorandum, dated January 31, 1949, talks about Los Alamos National Laboratory in New Mexico. This facility, which was established in 1943, was tasked to design nuclear weapons for the Manhattan Project. Obviously, this was a highly sensitive installation, and this memorandum outlines that UFOs were specifically "targeting" this facility. The memorandum, in part, states:

At recent Weekly Intelligence Conferences of G-2, ONI, 051, and FBI, in the Fourth Army Area, Officers of G-2, Fourth Army have discussed the matter of "Unidentified Aircraft" or "Unidentified Aerial Phenomena," otherwise known as "Flying Discs," "Flying Saucers," and "Balls of Fire." This matter is considered top secret by intelligence Officers of both the Army and the Air Forces.

It is well known that there have been during the past two years reports from the various parts of the country of the sighting of unidentified aerial objects which have been called in newspaper parlance "flying discs" and "flying saucers." The first such sightings were reported from Sweden, and it was thought that the objects, the nature of which was unknown, might have originated in Russia.

In July 1948, an unidentified aircraft was "seen" by an Eastern Airlines Pilot and co-pilot and one or more passengers of the Eastern Airlines plane over Montgomery, Alabama. This aircraft was reported to be of an unconventional type without wings and resembled generally a "rocket ship" of the type depicted in comic strips. It was reported to have had windows; to have been larger than the Eastern Airlines plane, and to have been traveling at an estimated speed of 2700 miles an hour. It appeared out of a thunderhead ahead of the Eastern Airlines plane and immediately disappeared in another cloud narrowly missing a collision with the Eastern Airlines plane. No sound or air disturbance was noted in connection with this appearance.

During the past two months various sightings of unexplained phenomena have been reported in the vicinity of the A.E.C. Installation at Los Alamos, New Mexico, where these phenomena now appear to be concentrated. During December 1948 on the 5th, 6th, 7th, 8th, 11th, 13th, 14th, 20th, and 28th, sightings of unexplained phenomena were made near Los Alamos by Special Agents of the Office of Special Investigations; Airline Pilots; Military Pilots; Los Alamos Security Inspectors; and private citizens. On January 6, 1949, another similar object was sighted in the same area.

It goes on to state:

There have been daytime sightings which are tentatively considered to possibly resemble the exhaust of some type of jet-propelled object. Night time sightings have taken the form of lights usually described as brilliant green, similar to a green traffic signal or green neon light. Some reports indicated that the light began and ended with a red or orange flash. Other reports have given the color as red, white, blue-white, and yellowish green. Trailing lights sometimes observed are said to be red. The spectrum analysis of one light indicates that it may be a copper compound of the type known to be used in rocket experiments and which completely disintegrates upon explosion, leaving no debris. It is noted that no debris has ever been known to be located anywhere resulting from the unexplained phenomena.

Recent observations have indicated that the unidentified phenomena travel at a rate of speed estimated at a minimum of three miles per second and a maximum of twelve miles a second, or 27,000 miles an hour. Their reported course indicates that they travel on an East-West line with probability that they approach from the

Northern quadrant, which would be the last stage of the great circle route if they originated in Russia. When observed they seem to be in level flight at a height of six to ten miles and thus traveling on a tangent to the earth's surface. They occasionally dip at the end of the path and on two occasions a definite vertical change in the path was indicated. These phenomena have not been known to have been sighted, however, at any intermediate point between Russia and Los Alamos, but only at the end of the flight toward the apparent "target," namely, Los Alamos.

Let's dissect this document for a moment. First, the record shows that the topic of UFOs and "unidentified aerial phenomena" was classified as "Top Secret." This does contradict many of the reports that have surfaced from the late 1940s, so this particular statement alone lends credence that there were many more UFO documents that existed back then, yet not released to the public. As proof of this, I refer you back to chapter 2, in which I recount a story that Wright-Patterson Air Force Base (WPAFB) found nearly one thousand pages on UFOs dated from 1948 and 1949, which encompasses the same year this memorandum was written. According to this FBI memorandum, there should be a majority of formerly "Top Secret" documents, but on the contrary, there were none.

The records that WPAFB released to me held either an "Unclassified" or formerly held a "Confidential" classification level but nothing higher. This is a crucial point when juxtaposed with this FBI memorandum. If the "matter was classified 'TOP SECRET'" as the document stated, then the majority of these records would have been formerly classified at that level or withheld from release if they were still currently classified. They were neither, and that fact supports there was or is much more to find on UFOs around this era. However, it could have been destroyed or hidden from public view.

Second, if you did not catch it, were the UFO characteristics outlined in the document. The line of most importance was that fact that whatever this unidentified phenomena was, it traveled at a maximum speed of 27,000 miles per hour.

How important is the fact that UFOs were estimated to go at top speeds of 27,000 miles per hour? Chuck Yeager broke the sound barrier just two years prior on October 14, 1947, when he flew the experimental Bell X-1 jet aircraft. That means he reached a top speed of Mach 1, or approximately 767 miles per hour, flying at an altitude of 45,000 feet.

In fact, it was not until November 16, 2004, that NASA broke a new record with their X-43 jet aircraft hitting speeds of Mach 9.6, or approximately 7,366 miles per hour. That means that after this FBI memorandum was written, speaking about a phenomenon that reached speeds of 27,000 miles per hour, it would take another fifty-five years for NASA to set an amazing speed record, and still, these UFOs back in 1949 were going more than three times the speed of NASA's X-43 in 2004. How is this even possible?

Skeptics may want to immediately argue that it was a radar glitch and nothing we should take seriously. However, the FBI memorandum does not reference a possible glitch at all and even rules out the only likely physical object that would travel at such speeds into Earth's atmosphere: meteorites. They end the memorandum stating the following:

> Some nine scientific reasons are stated to exist which indicated that the phenomena observed are not due to meteorites. The only conclusions reached thus far are that they are either hitherto unobserved natural phenomena or that they are man-made. No scientific experiments are known to exist in this country which could give rise to such phenomena.
>
> So, while flying saucers were being dismissed publicly as misidentifications, hoaxes, and the product of Saturday night drinking parties, the Army and Air Force looked upon the matter as "Top Secret."

This last part, for me, was the kicker. It showed clearly that publicly the story was wildly different then behind the scenes. To "Joe Q.," UFOs were being dismissed and became simply a drinking party topic of conversation, but behind the scenes, it held the highest classification the military could give it, and it remained unsolved and dangerous. It should be noted that I do not have a single "Top Secret" document related to a meteor entering the Earth's atmosphere.

Nuclear installation incursions never slowed through the decades. One record, undated, recounts an event at Francis E. Warren Air Force Base in Wyoming, on the night of July 31, 1965. This document, which is found in the Project Blue Book collection at the National Archives and Records Administration (NARA), details the encounter:

Subject: Unidentified Flying Objects (UFO)

1. Reference 200-2 as amended. Francis E. Warren Air Force Base is located in an area which has recently experienced a considerable number of reports pertaining to unidentified flying objects. On the night of 31 July 1965, several civilians in Cheyenne, Wyoming, reported to the local radio stations various objects generally with red and green flashing lights. These were relayed to the Francis E. Warren Command Post. All missile sites were immediately contacted and alerted to be on the watch for such objects. As a result, the following number of sightings were reported during the following three nights:

31 July	75 objects	observed by	70 personnel
1 August	29 objects	observed by	27 personnel
2 August	44 objects	observed by	46 personnel
Totals:	148 objects		143

2. Description of Objects: Reported objects are mostly round, although there are reports of oval/cigar-shaped and pencil-shaped, or merely a light source. Reported sizes vary from that of a pinhead to a nickel when seen with the naked eye, and from the size of a pea to a half-dollar when seen through binoculars. Where sightings involved more than one object, V-shaped, echelon, cross, box, and tail-shaped formations were reported. On August 1st, there was one daytime report, from a civilian source in Cheyenne, of an oblong object tumbling through the sky and in the distance becoming two objects before disappearing in separate directions. There were no discernable features, except that most reports stated that colored lights were flashing on and off at one to two second intervals, sometimes becoming alternately bright and dim. Possible tails were reported in a few cases. There has been no sound reported in association with any of the objects. All of the moving objects were to the northwest, north and northeast of the observation points.

In the 1960s, Warren Air Force Base was considered the first nuclear ICBM missile base in America. With this fact, Warren AFB would be one of the most highly secured and protected places within the borders of the United States, and yet, as indicated by this document, it was encroached upon by a number of unidentified objects over the course of three nights.

Another case, also recounted in the Project Blue Book files, occurred on October 24, 1968. This particular case occurred over Minot Air Force Base in North Dakota. The Project Blue Book case file on this incident stretched more than one hundred pages, which is rather large when compared to other individual reports. In part, this case file details the event:

At about 0300 hours local, a B-52 that was about 39 miles northwest of Minot AFB and was making practice penetrations sighted an unidentified blip on their radar. Initially the target traveled approximately 2 1/2 mile in 3 sec or at about 3,000 mi/hr. After passing from the right to the left of the plane it assumed a position off the left wing of the B-52. The blip stayed off the left wing for approximately 20 miles at which point it broke off. Scope photos were taken. When the target was close to the B-52 neither of the two transmitters in the B-52 would operate properly and when it broke off both returned to normal function.

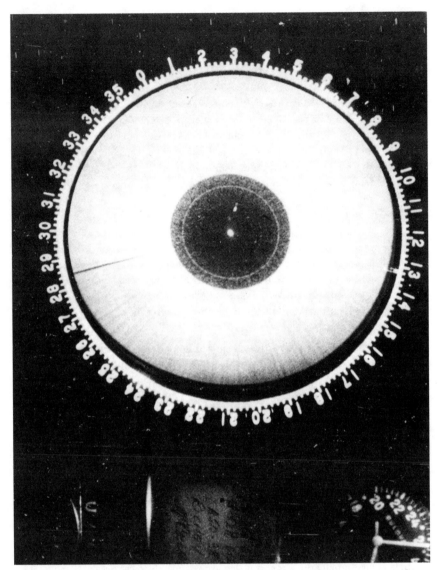

Figure 9.1. Example of the radar photographs taken when the screens were showing the UFO.

The document also stated:

Fourteen other people in separate locations also reported sighting a similar object. Also, at this approximate time, a security alarm for one of the sites was activated. This was an alarm for both the outer and inner ring. When guards arrived at the scene they found that the outer door was open and the combination lock on the inner door had been moved. The weather was generally misty, the temperature was 28–29 deg F and the wind 5–10 knots.

In addition to the case details, there were also multiple photographs that were taken by the radar operator of the radar screen to document the incident. These photographs confirm that not only were the UFOs being reported by physical observances, they were also being captured on radar.

Although there are many details in the more than one hundred pages in this case file, what is the most humorous is page 1, which held the "conclusion" by Project Blue Book staff on the Minot AFB UFO encounter. It reads:

The ground visual sightings appear to be of the star Sirius and the B-52, which was flying in the area. The B-52 radar contact and the temporary loss of the UHF transmission could be attributed to a plasma similar to ball lightning. The air visual from the B-52 could be the star Vega, which was on the horizon at the time, or it could be a light on the ground, or possibly a plasma.

PROJECT 10073 RECORD	
1. DATE - TIME GROUP 24/0030 24 Oct 68 24/0530Z	2. LOCATION Minot AFB, North Dakota
3. SOURCE Military	10. CONCLUSION Ground-Visual: 1. Probable (AIRCRAFT)(B-52) 2. Probable Astro (SIRIUS) Radar: Possible (PLASMA) Air-Visual: Possible (PLASMA)
4. NUMBER OF OBJECTS See Case	
5. LENGTH OF OBSERVATION 4 Hours, 48 Minutes	11. BRIEF SUMMARY AND ANALYSIS SEE CASE FILE
6. TYPE OF OBSERVATION Air-Radar, Air-Visual Ground-Visual	
7. COURSE See Case	COMMENTS: The ground visual sightings appear to be of the star Sirius and the B-52 which was flying the area. The B-52 radar contact and the temporary loss of UHF transmission could be attributed to plasma, similar to ball lighting. The air-visual from the B-52 could be the star Vega which was on the horizon at the time, or it could be a light on the ground, or possibly a plasma.
8. PHOTOS ☐ Yes XX No	
9. PHYSICAL EVIDENCE ☐ Yes XX No	
FORM FTD SEP 63 0-329 (TDE) Previous editions of this form may be used.	

Figure 9.2. A highly unlikely explanation for the Minot sighting.

At least fourteen people in different locations all mistook a star for a flying aircraft? In addition to the eyewitnesses, the radar operator, who was also highly trained, captured plasma or ball lightning at the exact same time all by chance and as a huge coincidence? The odds of all of those mistakes being made by so many people, all at the same time, would be so astronomical, it's laughable.

Another incident, popular in UFO literature, was a UFO event at Malmstrom Air Force Base in Montana. This story is often recalled by U.S. Air Force Captain (1st Lieutenant at the time of the event) Robert Salas. His testimony, which he has given on many occasions, says that on the night of the event, he was in charge of monitoring the readiness and security of the ten nuclear missiles that were under their command at the base.

Captain Salas was below ground when he received a call from the Flight Security Controller (FSC) topside. Capt. Salas was informed that the security team outside were observing unidentified "lights" in the sky that were making unusual maneuvers. They were traveling at a high velocity and would make directional changes.

As Capt. Salas was relaying the message to the Missile Combat Crew Commander, 1st Lieutenant Frederick Meiwald, all of the nuclear missiles began to go offline, one by one. Capt. Salas also recounts that some of the missile indicators had "security violation lights" illuminated, which possibly showed that there were possible incursions by something at those sites.

Capt. Salas also has testified, and sworn under affidavit, that the missiles remained offline until at least the time they were relieved by another crew the next morning. Capt. Salas was interviewed by the 490th Squadron Commander Colonel George Eldridge and another officer from the Air Force Office of Special Investigations (AFOSI) about the encounter. After the interview, Capt. Salas was informed the incident would be classified "Secret" and they were not to speak about it to any other person.

As recounted in a former classified "Secret" history of the 341st Strategic Missile Wing and 341st Combat Support Group, for the dates of January 1 through March 31, 1967, the story is confirmed.

On 16 March 1967 at 0845, all sites in Echo (E) Flight, Malmstrom AFB, shutdown with No-Go indications of Channel 9 and 12 on Voice Reporting Signal Assemble (VRSA). All LF's in E Flight lost strategic alert nearly simultaneously. No other Wing I configuration lost strategic alert at that time.

In this particular document, it recalls that there were rumors of UFO sightings at the base on this night, but they dismiss the claim. They state:

Rumors of Unidentified Flying Objects (UFO) around the area of Echo Flight during the time of the fault were disproven. A Mobile Strike Team, which had checked all November Flight's LF's on the morning of 16 March 67, were questions and stated that no unusual activity or sightings were observed.

It seems yet again the U.S. military was discounting testimony and fact and simply trying to explain away the UFO phenomenon. Capt. Salas's testimony has been signed under a sworn affidavit, and his details completely contradict the "final" report on what happened at Malmstrom AFB in 1967. One of the final lines pertaining to this incident, as stated in this declassified history, states:

> Due to the fact that the power tests were essentially negative, it appears that the cause of the Echo Flight problem was of the EMP or electrostatic nature.

If this was a lone incident, I may even dismiss it as being a coincidence and nothing of great interest. However, it is not. On the contrary, it is just one of many UFO encounters within sensitive airspace of military facilities housing nuclear weapons.

Intrigued by some of these stories, I decided to look a bit deeper into the connection between UFOs and nuclear weapons, if any. Documents from decades ago obviously existed, and they showed a steady number of cases, throughout the 1940s through at least the late 1970s, that proved the phenomenon was truly invading these sensitive airspaces, but what about more modern times?

So I filed a FOIA request to the Nuclear Regulatory Commission (NRC) for records pertaining to UFOs. My thought process was simple: if there was a connection between UFOs and these sensitive nuclear facilities, in addition to these historical documents, maybe there was something more recent. According to the NRC's official mission statement:

> The U.S. Nuclear Regulatory Commission (NRC) was created as an independent agency by Congress in 1974 to ensure the safe use of radioactive materials for beneficial civilian purposes while protecting people and the environment. The NRC regulates commercial nuclear power plants and other uses of nuclear materials, such as in nuclear medicine, through licensing, inspection and enforcement of its requirements.

I was surprised to receive what I did. It was not until February of 2017 that I first submitted this request to the NRC regarding UFOs, and to be quite honest, I expected a "no records" response, meaning, if anything did exist, it was transferred out to the National Archives and was no longer of interest to that specific agency. It did not take more than a month for the agency to respond, and as a result of the request, I obtained more than forty pages of documents.

Pages near the top of the stack introduced me to a never-before-heard-about encounter over a nuclear facility. It was a UFO encounter that occurred between 1986 and 1989, over Cooper Nuclear Station in Nebraska. Although not a nuclear missile base, Cooper Nuclear Station was what is known as a "boiling water reactor" type of nuclear power plant. Although this facility does not house ICBM missiles for the Air Force, it was still a highly secured area and had power nuclear reactors within the walls.

This UFO story is documented in a "Branch Evaluation, Plan & Recommendation" document, dated June 29, 2010. The back story was that a former security guard working at Cooper Nuclear Station in the mid- to late 1980s (identity is redacted in the record release) witnessed a UFO over the facility over the course of multiple nights. This security guard never reported the event and, in 2010, could not keep it quiet anymore. This document chronicles the entire story submitted:

> Concern: [a concern is one or two sentences]
> Sometimes between 1986 and 1989, an Unidentified Flying Object (UFO) violated the protected Cooper Nuclear Station and was not reported to the NRC as required.
> Concern Background, Supporting Information, & Comments:
> The CI described an event that occurred during his employment as a security officer at Cooper Nuclear Station. He was employed there from 1986 through 1989 and did not remember specifically when during that time the event occurred.
>
> While posted at the intake structure one night, he observed an "unidentified flying object" fly down the Missouri River about 150 feet in the air and hover in front of the intake. He observed it for a few moments and then contacted a fellow security officer who also observed it (he could not recall the individual's name exactly but his first name was [REDACTED] and his last name was either [REDACTED] [REDACTED]. After they together observed the UFO, it turned and went back up the river and did not come back that shift. He and the other officer shared their observation with their peers who did not believe them.
>
> The next evening he again was posted at the intake and observed the UFO return again. This time he didn't call anyone until the UFO had traversed into the protected area and hovered above the protected area just north of the Reactor Building. He said it was roughly triangular in shape with a circle of rotating lights on the bottom. He could not hear any propulsion noise from the UFO. He believes that it was roughly 1/3 the size of the Reactor Building. Once the UFO hovered in the protected area, he called the security break room and most of the officers on shift observed the UFO. These individuals included [REDACTED] [REDACTED] [REDACTED] and

ALLEGATION RECEIPT FORM

Allegation Number: RIV- 2010-A-0101

Facility/Outside Org Name:	Cooper Nuclear Station	Receipt Date:	June 13, 2010
Received By:	(b)(7)(C)		

CONCERN   1.

Concern: (A concern is one or two sentences.)

An unidentified flying object violated the protected area at Cooper Nuclear Station sometime between 1986 and 1989, but the event was not reported to the NRC as required.

Concern Details and Comments: Background material, supporting information, etc. Narrative concern description. What occurred? When did it occur? Where did it occur (location)? How/why did it occur?

The CI described an event that occurred during his employment as a security officer at Cooper Nuclear Station. He was employed there from 1986 through 1989 and did not remember specifically when during that time the event occurred.

While posted at the intake structure one night, he observed an "unidentified flying object" fly down the Missouri River about 150 feet in the air and hover in front of the intake. He observed it for a few moments and then contacted a fellow security officer who also observed it (he could not recall the individual's name exactly but his first name was (b)(7)(and his last name was either (b)(7)(C) . After they together observed the UFO, it turned and went back up the river and did not come back that shift. He and the other officer shared their observation with their peers who did not believe them.

The next evening he again was posted at the intake and observed the UFO return again. This time he didn't call anyone until the UFO had traversed into the protected area and hovered above the protected area just north of the Reactor Building. He said it was roughly triangular in shape with a circle of rotating lights on the bottom. He could not hear any propulsion noise from the UFO. He believes that it was roughly 1/3 the size of the Reactor Building. Once the UFO hovered in the protected area, he called the security break room and most of the officers on shift observed the UFO. These individuals included (b)(7)(C) and (b)(7)(C) (both of whom were security officers), all of whom still work at the plant today. After hovering there for a few minutes, the UFO exited the protected are and returned back up the river to the north as it had the previous night. The CI said that he never saw the UFO at the plant again after that evening.

The CI believes that this incident should have been reported as a violation of the protected area space but was not reported.

What other individuals (witnesses or other sources) could the NRC contact for information?

(b)(7)(C)

What records, documents, or other evidence should the NRC review?

Corrective action program entries from 1986-1989, security shift logs.

What is the potential safety impact? Is this an ongoing concern? Is it an immediate safety or security concern? If the concern is an immediate and/or ongoing concern, the issue must be called in promptly to your Branch Chief.

This is not an ongoing concern. No potential safety impact.

Was the concern brought to management's attention? Was it entered into the Corrective Actions Program (CAP#)? What actions have been taken? If not, why not?

The concern was brought to the attention of the security (b)(7)(C)   The CI thinks it might have been entered

Figure 9.3.   The official "Allegation Receipt Form," dated June 13, 2010, which documented the UFO encounter over Cooper Nuclear Station.

[REDACTED] (both of whom were security officers), all of whom still work at the plant today. After hovering there for a few minutes, the UFO exited the protected area and returned back up the river to the north as it had the previous night. The CI said that he never saw the UFO at the plant again after that evening.

The CI believes that this incident should have been reported as a violation of the protected area space but was not reported.

8/23/10 UPDATE: The SRI at Cooper conducted a search of the corrective action program between 1/1/1986–12/31/1989 using the words: "ufo," "flying," "unidentified," "protected area," and "hover." The search yielded no entries associated with this concern.

Although this is interesting, what was next in the packet drove home the importance of documenting the UFO encounter. Just a friendly reminder, this was an event that occurred in the mid- to late 1980s and was submitted to the NRC in 2010. That means that more than forty years have passed since the U.S. government has denounced interest in UFO-related events. Yet the NRC took this testimony and drafted a report to be sent to Cooper Nuclear Station, now owned by the Nebraska Public Power District. In a letter dated July 27, 2010, from the NRC to the chief nuclear officer at Cooper Nuclear Station, it is stated:

SUBJECT: REFERRAL INFORMATION
REFERENCE: ALLEGATION RIV-2010-A-0101
Dear. Mr. O'Grady:
The U.S. Nuclear Regulatory Commission recently received information concerning activities at the Cooper Nuclear Station. We are providing this information described in this letter for your evaluation. Specifically, sometime between 1986 and 1989, an Unidentified Flying Object (UFO) violated the protected area at the Cooper Nuclear Station, was allegedly witnessed by security officers, and was not reported to the NRC, as required.
No response to this letter is requested. This letter should be controlled and distribution limited to personnel with a "need to know." Please contact Ms. Bernadette Baca, Senior Allegations Coordinator, Region IV, at (817) 860-8245 with any additional questions you may have concerning this information.

Attached to this letter was the "Branch Evaluation, Plan & Recommendation" referenced above. As you can see, there was a "need to know" basis for anyone being told about this particular UFO incident. It seemed, by the tone of this letter and the attached report, that even in 2010 the NRC was taking the topic seriously enough to report it and make sure that the present-day facility was aware of the event.

Another key part of this story was the "fact checking" done by the NRC within the "Corrective Action Program" or CAP. In this particular database, the NRC checked to see whether keywords relating to UFOs through this time frame came up, and they did not. Meaning, if you read the "Branch Evaluation, Plan & Recommendation" document above and notice the "update" paragraph toward the end, it was referenced that "no entries associated with this concern" were found.

However, with the way I worded my FOIA request, I was able to retrieve all of the documents relating to this particular event, not just these reports. I also received e-mails. Another record confirms that although they did not find anything in the CAP database relating to the UFO encounter, it actually may not mean they did not see anything at the time regarding the encounter. In an e-mail, also released under this FOIA request, sent from Nick Taylor, the senior resident inspector at Cooper Nuclear Station to Jesse Rollins, senior allegation specialist and physical security inspector with the NRC, it states:

Jesse,
Sorry I missed your call. We're working weird hours at Cooper right now due to flooding, ongoing event on site.
I did some searching of the records in the corrective action program. I searched for hits between 11/1/1986 and 12/31/1989 for the following words and did not find any hits that sounded remotely close to what you are looking for:
"ufo"
"flying"
"unidentified"
"protected area"
"hover"
If you can think of any other word searches you want me to try, let me know.
One precaution—I'd be careful about concluding that if an event wasn't recorded in CAP that it didn't occur. Corrective action program implementation in the late 1980's was nothing like what it is now. Case in point—only 1020 condition reports were written in the time frame 1/1/1986–12/31/1989. By contrast Cooper documents almost 10,000 condition reports per year in the modem day. It's entirely possible that an event could have occurred in the late 1980's and we would find no record of it in CAP.
Hope that helps,
Nick Taylor
Senior Resident Inspector, USNRC, Cooper Nuclear Station

The stack of records from the NRC went from interesting to bizarre. The above case at Cooper Nuclear Station had never been released publicly before. However, what came next were some incredibly strange "allegation" documents that the NRC received. For example, one claim submitted to the NRC in 1998 was recorded as the following:

The individual expressed vague concerns about finding low-level radiation within the last year where his daughter, whom he believes is an alien or alien transplant, passed. In addition, the individual believes that travel speed can be increased using the relativity equation with minor modifications. Finally, the individual has observed UFOs.

This particular case was closed after the "alleger" was sent a letter dated December 29, 1998. In this, the NRC stated:

We have reviewed your letter and determined that the issues, as described, do not appear to be within the jurisdiction of the U.S. Nuclear Regulatory Commission (NRC), and that further action by the NRC is not appropriate.

Another "allegation," from 1997, said the following:

A letter alleges that the DOD has been flying nuclear powered crafts from the area for over 50 years. The USAF refers to the crafts as UFOs. Several of the test crafts have crashed, contaminating sites in New Mexico.

The NRC did offer a follow-up letter but said anything relating to this allegation, as they stated in the above, would be "not within jurisdiction of the NRC" and the case was closed.

I bring these two latter "allegations" up because it shows that if a case holds no merit, is a wild claim, or is not of interest, the NRC does not do anything with the report. I also include these so you can contrast the actions by the NRC when compared to the Cooper Nuclear Station UFO incident. That was obviously taken very seriously, followed up, and given a "need to know" basis for access to the story. These others were simply dismissed, and the unnamed individuals submitting the allegations were sent a courteous letter, but no action was taken further.

These records solidified that there was a connection, which came years after those incidents documented decades prior that occurred toward the present day. It also confirmed the interest that the U.S. government had in these reports and that they would continue to "take action" to ensure the incidents were documented and the people with a "need to know" would be informed.

Possibly the most terrifying discovery, which will then make all of the previous records documenting UFO encounters near nuclear weapons more important, was a discovery I made in 2001 within documents at the CIA. I had briefly seen reference to an incident where an unidentified object was seen by Russian radar crews in January of 1995. By definition, it was a UFO, and they wrongfully assumed it was an incoming ICBM ballistic missile.

Although the Cold War had officially ended, tensions still ran hot. When I requested information about the incident from the CIA in 2000, they partially released the "Report of the Commission to Assess the Ballistic Missile Threat to the United States," which was written July 15, 1998. This record recounted one of the closest incidents we came to World War III, and it was all caused by a UFO:

> The most serious incident demonstrating the acute pressure on the command system under the short time constraints and the system's susceptibility to false warning occurred only three years ago. In January 1995, Russian radars detected and began tracking one or more apparent missiles fired from a spot near the coast of Norway. Interpreted as a possible attack by a Western missile submarine, the nuclear command system started the countdown to a launch decision for the first time in its history. The event activated President Yeltsin's nuclear suitcase and triggered an emergency teleconference between him and his nuclear advisors. About eight minutes elapsed, only a couple of minutes short of the procedural deadline for reaching a decision to launch on warning, before determining that the missile posed no threat to Russia. As it turned out, the missile was a U.S. scientific rocket launched from an island off the Norwegian coast to study the Northern Lights.

This incident shows how Russia was just minutes away from firing a retaliatory strike. The entire event was sparked by an unknown object flying in the air that was misidentified and therefore considered an aggressive maneuver. Thankfully, this particular situation worked out, and nothing drastic happened. In the end, it was not a true "UFO" as it was identified as a rocket—it was just that no one informed the Russian radar crew to watch out for it and not be alarmed. This document should be a lesson on how countries react to unknown craft or blips on a radar screen and how dangerous the unknown really is.

This declassified CIA document reinforces the need to solve the UFO problem or, if nothing else, create better detection capabilities so false alarms, weather inversions, or the simple launch of a satellite do not cause World War III. Now go back and re-read all of the other encounters that I outlined in just this chapter. These incidents that remained "unidentified" could have been *much* worse.

Could the connection between UFOs and nuclear incidents and installations be the key to unraveling this mystery? With a clearly heavily classified topic, and documents remaining largely redacted, it is unclear. However, my fight for UFO records would strengthen the absolute threat to national security along with the need for secrecy. It would just take me years to figure out what lengths they would go to in order to cover it all up.

THE REASON
FOR SECRECY

The Defense Intelligence Agency (DIA), the Office of the Assistant Secretary of Defense (OASD), and the Nuclear Regulatory Commission (NRC) really drive home the national security issue. Documents exist that detail UFO encounters throughout the globe and in America alike. The UFO phenomenon, no matter what it was, seemed to hold no preference on where or to whom it would appear.

These documents that I have gone over in the previous chapters completely contradict the "company line." In one breath, the U.S. government states there is "no national security threat," yet in the next breath, they release detailed cases that clearly show we are in danger.

With this evidence, the biggest question is: why? Another intelligence agency in particular really highlights not only the reason why they are covering it up, but how "Top Secret" the information remains, and that is the National Security Agency (NSA).

Before Edward Snowden, not many people paid attention to the NSA. We know them now as the intelligence agency that eavesdrops on our phone calls, e-mails, and probably whatever device they can tap into to hear our everyday conversations. Beyond that, the NSA's mission goes much deeper and dives into much more sinister territory than just listening to our phone calls.

According to their mission statement:

The National Security Agency/Central Security Service (NSA/CSS) leads the U.S. Government in cryptology that encompasses both Signals Intelligence (SIGINT) and Information Assurance (IA) products and services, and enables

Computer Network Operations (CNO) in order to gain a decision advantage for the Nation and our allies under all circumstances.

But what exactly does that mean?

Like many government agencies, their online mission statements make them sound much more harmless than they really are. As the Snowden revelations revealed, the NSA has undertaken some very intrusive operations, even against the American citizens they aim to protect. In addition to all of that, they also have a deep and long history with the UFO phenomenon.

Around 1979, the "Citizens Against UFO Secrecy" or CAUS, asked the NSA for UFO documents under the FOIA but was denied access to them. In total, the NSA discovered there were two hundred and thirty-nine documents responsive to their request. Seventy-nine of those had originated from other agencies, so as mandated by the FOIA, these particular documents were forwarded to those other agencies for review and release. This particular action of forwarding records to another agency is quite common when using the FOIA. For example, many intelligence reports or other documents originate from one agency but are forwarded to many others for their intelligence purposes. Thankfully, agencies do communicate to a point with each other, but during the course of a FOIA request, if one of these documents is found but determined to be written by another agency, that other agency is what is called the "Office of Primary Responsibility" or OPR. No government agency can declassify information or documents that originated from other agencies. In this case, seventy-nine of the UFO records were forwarded out for review and possible release.

The remaining UFO records, originating from within the NSA, were also reviewed for release. Very few actually were sent to CAUS, and the remaining number of records remained classified and withheld. I will go over some of the UFO records that have been released over the years later in this chapter, but I wanted to start out with this particular FOIA request by CAUS as it escalated into a courtroom.

The step of taking a government agency into a courtroom is a right afforded to anyone utilizing the FOIA. In short, the progression to this stage is: First you file a FOIA request. If you disagree with the release (or lack of release) of information, you can then go to step number two, which is to appeal that decision. If you are denied your appeal, the third and final step afforded to us all is that you can sue under the FOIA and make your case in front of the judge.

CAUS v. NSA is incredibly important because this reveals, quite literally, the reason "why" the NSA withheld their UFO records. During the course of this case, CAUS submitted to the judge their argument for the release of the

NSA UFO-related documentation. In response, the NSA created two affidavits to explain the reasons why the UFO information was to be withheld from the public, as they would not budge on their decision to not release the information into the public domain.

The affidavits were written by the chief officer of policy for the NSA, Eugene F. Yeates. The first of the two was considered the "Unclassified" version. This version was released to CAUS and the public, and that was intended to adequately explain the reason for withholding the information. What was not in this unclassified version was any information that would put "national security" information at risk. In other words, it was a softened-down version of the real reasons they were not really going to give the public their UFO documents.

The second affidavit was for the judge only. This particular document was classified "Top Secret" and was handed to the judge to explain, in national security–threatening detail, why the UFO information was not to be released. However, judges do not have appropriate clearances to just read any and all classified information. So in order for them to do so, they are given what is called an "in camera" (legal term meaning in private or in chambers) clearance. This will then allow them to read the "Top Secret" material in the affidavit. This allows them to review the appropriate information to make an adequate and informed decision, but that sensitive information is not released to the public during the course of the court case.

In the end, the judge sided with the NSA after reviewing the "Top Secret" version of the affidavit. The judge agreed that the information should be withheld and should stay locked up away from the curious minds of the general public.

In time, that affidavit was also requested under the FOIA. It was eventually released in the early 1990s, but the original version the NSA sent out spoke volumes about how sensitive the UFO-related documents really were.

Not much can be gleamed from a record that is primarily blacked out and redacted, but that in itself told an amazing story. It showed that whatever these UFO records were, they were classified, and they would remain so at the "Top Secret" level even more than a decade after the affidavit was written.

The release of these affidavits explained that the majority of the withheld documents related to Communications Intelligence, or COMINT. COMINT primarily contains information that is derived from the interception of foreign communications. According to the original release of the "Top Secret" Yeates affidavit:

One hundred and fifteen of these reports were produced by the signals intelligence organization [REDACTED][REDACTED]. These COMINT reports are provided to NSA [REDACTED][REDACTED].

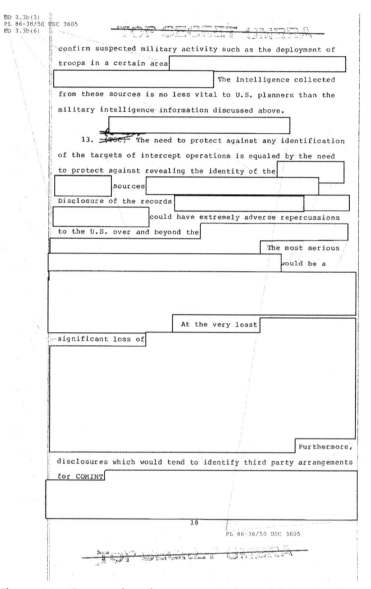

TOP SECRET UMBRA

confirm suspected military activity such as the deployment of
troops in a certain area

The intelligence collected
from these sources is no less vital to U.S. planners than the
military intelligence information discussed above.

13. (TSC) The need to protect against any identification
of the targets of intercept operations is equaled by the need
to protect against revealing the identity of the

sources

Disclosure of the records

could have extremely adverse repercussions
to the U.S. over and beyond the

The most serious

would be a

At the very least

significant loss of

Furthermore,
disclosures which would tend to identify third party arrangements
for COMINT

18

TOP SECRET UMBRA

Figure 10.1.   One page from the most recent release of the Yeates affidavit, clearly showing much is still withheld for "national security" reasons.

This is then followed by an entire paragraph that is blacked out. In fact, the entire page is sparse with words that are actually readable, but you can determine that the majority of the UFO-related documents withheld were COMINT reports and were collected from unnamed countries or sources. To be fair, the actual sources of the information *would be* properly classified, and I really do not necessarily disagree with them withholding that information. In intelligence terms, they call this "sources and methods." In other words, it is where they got the information from and how they received it.

Looking beyond that necessity of classifying that information, it is the pure fact they are collecting UFO intelligence at all that becomes incredibly important. What was even more interesting was *when* they were collecting it. The "Top Secret" Yeates affidavit explains:

> The remaining one hundred and fifty six records being withheld are communication intelligence (COMINT) reports which were produced between 1958 and 1979.

This fact contradicts the entire "company line" yet again. In 1969, those COMINT reports and intelligence papers should have ceased to exist altogether. Also recall this affidavit was written in 1980, so the fact that it is stated they go up to 1979 essentially means that they were actively collecting this UFO intelligence, and they had never stopped at any time.

Despite the COMINT reports being entirely withheld, the affidavit does reference a few documents the NSA did release at the time. One such record was entitled "UFO Hypothesis and Survival Questions." This was a "draft" document, classified "Secret" when it was written in 1968, toward the end of Project Blue Book. It explored multiple explanations for the UFO phenomenon. It started off with a statement about why the document was written in the first place:

> It is the purpose of this monograph to consider briefly some of the human survival implications suggested by the various principle hypothesis concerning the nature of the phenomena loosely categorized as U F O.

It then went on to explain various explanations for the UFO phenomenon; for example, it proposed the following: "All UFOs Are Hoaxes," "All UFOs Are Hallucinations," and "Some UFOs Are Secret Earth Projects." Each of these headings had breakdown explanations, with cited sources, and at first the record does appear to be a complete debunking job on explaining away UFOs. However, that was not the case as the author of the record then entertained this idea: "Some UFOs Are Related to Extra-Terrestrial Intelligence."

The author broke it down this way:

According to some eminent scientists closely associated with the study of this phenomenon, this hypothesis cannot be disregarded. (The well documented sightings over Washington, D.C. in 1952 strongly support his view.) This hypothesis has a number of far-reaching human survival implications:

a. If "they" discover you, it is an old but hardly invalid rule of thumb, "they" are your technological superiors. Human history has shown us time and again the tragic results of a confrontation between a technologically superior civilization and a technologically inferior people. The "inferior" is usually subject to physical conquest.

b. Often in the past, a technologically superior people are also possessors of a more virile or aggressive culture. In a confrontation between two peoples of significantly different culture levels, those having the inferior or less virile culture most often suffer a tragic loss of identity and are absorbed by the other people.

c. Some peoples who were technologically and/or culturally inferior to other nations have survived—have maintained their identity—have equalized the differences between them and their adversaries. The Japanese people have given us an excellent example of the methods required to achieve such survival:

(1) full and honest acceptance of the nature of the inferiorities separating you from the advantages of the other peoples,

(2) complete national solidarity in all positions taken in dealing with the other culture,

(3) highly controlled and limited intercourse with the other side—doing only those things advantageous to the foreigner which you are absolutely forced to do by the circumstances,

(4) a correct but friendly attitude toward the other people,

(5) a national eagerness to learn everything possible about the other citizens—its technological and cultural strengths and weaknesses. This often involves sending selected groups and individuals to the other's country to become one of his kind, or even to help him in his wars against other adversaries.

(6) adopting as many of the advantages of the opposing people as you can, and doing it as fast as possible—while still protecting your own identity by molding each new knowledge increment into your own cultural cast.

In one of the supporting footnotes, a familiar name was also cited:

12. Professor James E Macdonald, Astronomer, Professor Allen J. Hynek, Astrophysicist, Jacques Vallee, Astronomer, Seymour Hess, Astronomer, etc. [statement] that some of these objects are probably EXTRATERRESTRIAL in

~~SECRET~~ DRAFT *clean copy*

SUBJECT: UFO's and the Intelligence Community Blind Spot to Surprise or Deceptive Data

1. The implications of the UFO phenomena go far beyond the particular phenomena itself. The human incapacity to objectively process such data indicates a serious weakness in the intelligence community. This weakness ought to be remedied and quickly if the United States is to be able to respond swiftly and appropriately to surprise attack indicators. The reason that surprise attack is such a basic ingredient of military success is that it is able to rely on a most dependable human blind spot. The inability of most men to objectively process and evaluate highly unusual data and to react to the data in a meaningful way.

2. Scientific Findings: Dr. Jacques Vallee* famed communications science expert has studied thousands of cases where human beings have observed unusual phenomena. He has found that the human response to such observation is predictable and graphically depictable. Whether the person's psychological structure is being assaulted by the unusual and shocking brutality of a murder or the strangeness of a UFO sighting the effect is the same:

    a. Initially as by a kind of psychological inertia, the mind records fairly objectively what the eye is reporting.*

    b. But when it has realized the strange nature of the phenomena it goes into shock. The mind likes to live in a comfortable world where it feels it knows what to expect, and that, is not too threatening either physically or psychologically. The unusual dispells the comfortable illusion the mind has created. This shock tears at the very mooring of the human psychological structure.*

    c. To protect itself against such an intrusive and threatening reality the mind will begin to add imagination and interpretation to the incoming data to make it more acceptable. Since the mind is doing all this in haste some of the hurridly aided details and suggestions tumble over one another and contradict one another in a bizzare fashion (as any police officer interrogating murder witnesses will tell you*) (See Chart A).

    d. Once the mind has constructed a "safe" framework for the new information it may again peek out and collect some more objective data. If the data is still threatening it will again go into shock and the process starts all over again.*

    e. If the data is at the highest strangeness level where it brings terror either:

        (1) The mind will pass out and go into amnesia burying the events perhaps permanently in the unconscious.*

~~SECRET~~ DRAFT

Figure 10.2. One of the pages showing the clear classification that the document "UFO's and the Intelligence Community Blind Spot to Surprise or Deceptive Data" still holds.

origin is also supported by a 1958 report by Brazilian sailors [UNREADABLE] scientific investigators.

It seems that even in 1968, the year the record was written, this author did not fully discount the scientists who came forward and their belief in the extraterrestrial hypothesis.

The Yeates affidavit also mentioned a second (non-COMINT) record that was released. The author's name was protected from disclosure, so therefore it was redacted, but this document was titled "UFO's and the Intelligence Community Blind Spot to Surprise or Deceptive Data." The date it was written is believed to be circa 1968 as well, but the document lacks a specific year so it is unclear. It was also classified "Secret" at the time it was written, and it begins:

> The implications of the UFO phenomena go far beyond the particular phenomena itself. The human incapacity to objectively process such data indicates a serious weakness in the intelligence community. This weakness ought to be remedied and quickly if the United States is to be able to respond swiftly and appropriately to surprise attack indicators. The reason that surprise attack is such a basic ingredient of military success is that it is able to rely on a most dependable human blind spot: The inability of most men to objectively process and evaluate highly unusual data and to react to the data in a meaningful way.

I believe these drafts by this unknown NSA author prove that even toward the end of Project Blue Book, the intelligence community was not discounting the extraterrestrial connection with the UFO phenomenon, but also they knew that the phenomenon itself was a huge threat on multiple levels. This is indicative by the writing, tone, and possible explanations eluding to the extraterrestrial connection.

Although these few records were released, the "Top Secret" affidavit's primary purpose was to explain to the judge the reasons for the remaining COMINT documents to be withheld. That was ultimately what CAUS was fighting for, but they failed to convince the judge to have the NSA release them. They lost the case so the documents remained "Top Secret" and hidden from us all.

As the years went on from this court case, the NSA would release these select few records I referenced to all requesters that asked for them, but they continued to withhold the hundreds of pages of COMINT reports. In my opinion, these intelligence papers may hold at least one key to understanding the UFO phenomenon.

Now, fast-forward to 1996, and my battle began with the NSA. In my original launching of The Black Vault, I was hitting every government agency

I could find, including the NSA, requesting UFO information. Of course, I got the above-mentioned documents, a copy of the heavily redacted Yeates affidavit, and the "Unclassified" version of the same. In addition to this, I actually received quite a few more pages that appeared not to have been released to CAUS in 1979/1980. Sadly, however, the NSA was still hiding the hundreds of pages of COMINT reports even after all these years had passed since CAUS was originally denied and had their day in court.

Some of this additional material included some rather strange additions, like article clippings from the *National Enquirer* and the *New York Times*, both about UFOs. It also included an article about a French UFO study and additional photocopies of articles published by various UFO investigators and non-NSA personnel. Despite this information not being anything "Top Secret"—it was rather strange that the NSA was collecting and archiving these types of newspaper articles and written research papers by UFO investigators. One was written by Peter Gersten, the lawyer for CAUS during the aforementioned lawsuit and was published by *Frontiers of Science* magazine.

Although it was very strange that those articles were being archived by the NSA, this batch of records released to me went far beyond a few newspaper clippings and articles that the NSA had collected. One of the most interesting was a document entitled "Key to Extraterrestrial Messages" by H. Campaigne. This was an "unclassified" document and was originally published in *NSA Technical Journal*, volume XIV, number 1. The *NSA Technical Journal* began in 1954 and internally published various articles for dissemination to NSA personnel. Although this specific record was "unclassified," many issues of the *NSA Technical Journal* remain classified at various levels, and although the FOIA has produced some of them after requests were filed, many remain hidden due to their sensitive nature.

The "Key to Extraterrestrial Messages" article by H. Campaigne outlined how to decipher alien messages and even listed alien messages in the article. It is a companion piece that went with another titled "Extraterrestrial Intelligence." This particular document, seemingly published first, began with an intriguing introduction:

> Recently a series of radio messages was heard coming from outer space. The transmission was not continuous but was cut by pauses into pieces which could be taken as units, for they were repeated over and over again.

The "Key to the Extraterrestrial Messages" was just that: a key to decoding these messages from an intelligent species in the cosmos. The NSA claims the

AV $\cdot$ 45 and 66 $\cdot$ AV $\cdots$ BL$_{11}$ belongs to JR$_5$;
AV $\cdot$ 67 and 126 $\cdot$ AV $\cdot$ $\cdot$ BL$_{12}$ belongs to JR$_6$;
AV $\cdot$ 127 and 142 $\cdot$ AV $\cdots$ BL$_{11}$ belongs to JR$_7$;
The set BL$_1$, BL$_8$, BL$_{16}$, BL$_{26}$, BL$_5$, BL$_{67}$, BL$_{127}$ belongs to JO$_1$;
The set BL$_2$, BL$_9$, BL$_{11}$, BL$_{21}$, BL$_{46}$, BL$_{70}$, BL$_{110}$ belongs to JO$_2$;
The set BL$_5$, BL$_{15}$, BL$_{17}$, BL$_{61}$, BL$_{121}$ belongs to JO$_3$;
The set BL$_{16}$ and BL$_{46}$ and BL$_{10}$ and BL$_{62}$ and BL$_{122}$ belongs to JO$_4$;
The set BL$_2$, BL$_{17}$, BL$_{11}$, BL$_{63}$, BL$_{123}$ belongs to JO$_5$;
The set BL$_{10}$, BL$_{20}$, BL$_{42}$, BL$_{61}$, BL$_{124}$ belongs to JO$_6$ |note a garble
here, an N is repeated |;
The set BL$_{11}$, BL$_{42}$, BL$_{44}$, BL$_{64}$, BL$_{125}$ belongs to JO$_7$;
The set BL$_{42}$, BL$_{43}$, BL$_{11}$, BL$_{66}$, BL$_{126}$ belongs to JO$_{10}$;
The set BL$_{22}$, BL$_3$, BL$_{43}$, BL$_{42}$, BL$_{33}$, BL$_{41}$, BL$_{33}$, BL$_{36}$, BL$_{37}$, BL$_{100}$,
BL$_{101}$, BL$_{102}$, BL$_{104}$, BL$_{101}$, BL$_{106}$, BL$_{108}$, BL$_{103}$, BL$_{110}$, BL$_{112}$, BL$_{113}$,
BL$_{114}$, BL$_{116}$, BL$_{117}$, BL$_{112}$, BL$_{110}$, BL$_{111}$, BL$_{112}$ belongs to JO$_{11}$;
BL$_{16}$ and BL$_{20}$ and BL$_{110}$ belongs to JO$_{12}$;
The set BL$_{27}$, BL$_{54}$, BL$_{111}$ belongs to JO$_{13}$;
The set BL$_{30}$, BL$_{55}$, BL$_{112}$ belongs to JO$_{14}$;
The set BL$_{31}$, BL$_{56}$, BL$_{111}$ belongs to JO$_{15}$;
The set BL$_{32}$, BL$_{51}$, BL$_{111}$ belongs to JO$_{16}$;
The set BL$_{14}$, BL$_{57}$, BL$_{113}$ belongs to JO$_{17}$;
The set BL$_{31}$, BL$_{58}$, BL$_{116}$ belongs to JO$_{20}$;
The set BL$_{35}$, BL$_{57}$, BL$_{111}$ belongs to JO$_{21}$;
The set BL$_{36}$, BL$_{60}$, BL$_{120}$ belongs to JO$_{22}$;
CHAV belongs to KSPV.

The transcription leaves a lot to be resolved. There are several words
the meanings of which are yet to be determined. The word CHAV (or
CH$_0$) seems to be central. There are seven words JR$_i$ and eighteen
words JO$_j$ and each of these belongs to CHAV. There are 98 words BL$_{ij}$,
each of which seems to belong to a unique JO$_j$. Does each also belong to a
unique JR$_i$? With this hint we can straighten out the garbled message
above; it reads "0 < AV and AV < 22 = $\cdot$ JO$_{11}$ belongs to CHAV";
there was a V omitted. I was also able to reparse six other messages. I
will not bore you with the details, since the list above has been
corrected.

Since each BL$_{ij}$ belongs to one JR$_i$ and JO$_j$, these can be displayed in
a matrix

	JR$_1$	JR$_2$	JR$_3$	JR$_4$	JR$_5$	JR$_6$	JR$_7$
JO$_1$	BL$_1$	BL$_8$	BL$_{16}$	BL$_{26}$	BL$_{45}$	BL$_{67}$	BL$_{127}$
JO$_2$	BL$_2$	BL$_9$	BL$_{11}$	BL$_{21}$	BL$_{46}$	BL$_{70}$	BL$_{110}$
JO$_3$		BL$_5$	BL$_{15}$	BL$_{47}$	BL$_{61}$	BL$_{121}$	
JO$_4$		BL$_6$	BL$_{16}$	BL$_{10}$	BL$_{62}$	BL$_{122}$	
JO$_5$		BL$_7$	BL$_{17}$	BL$_{11}$	BL$_{63}$	BL$_{123}$	
JO$_6$		BL$_{10}$	BL$_{20}$	BL$_{42}$	BL$_{64}$	BL$_{124}$	

Figure 10.3. Some of the "alien codes" used in the "Key to the
Extraterrestrial Messages" document.

two records were simply "training exercises" for decoding *real* alien messages should the people of Earth ever receive them. Although I do not believe this was a real alien message, and I do believe it probably was a practice run if that ever did happen, it showed in a rather esoteric way that NSA analysts were practicing for such a scenario to unfold.

One other record released that is worth mentioning ties back to the 1976 Iran Incident I outlined in chapter 7. If you recall, I explained that the amazing story recounted in this four-page document was "unclassified." That in itself proved an amazing story, but within the NSA archives was another copy of an intelligence report regarding that same incident.

However, this particular document had a crossed-out "Secret" stamp on every page. Next to that was a crossed-out "Confidential" stamp, which then was followed by a "Declassify on" stamp. What this shows is the progression of classification to this particular intelligence report over time. When it was written, it was considered "Secret," the next level down from the highest classification of "Top Secret." In time the document was downgraded to a "Confidential" level and then later declassified to the public in 1981.

So why would the original report on the 1976 Iran Incident be "Unclassified" while this one was classified "Secret"? The biggest difference that I could find in this "Secret" version was an introduction at the top written by a U.S. Air Force pilot by the name of Captain Henry S. Shields. He stated:

> Sometime in his career, each pilot can expect to encounter strange, unusual happenings which will never be adequately or entirely explained by logic or subsequent investigation. The following article recounts such an episode as reported by two F-4 Phantom crews of the Imperial Iranian Air Force during late 1976. No additional information or explanation of the strange events has been forthcoming; the story will be filed away and probably forgotten, but it makes interesting, and possibly disturbing, reading.

The remainder of the document, presumably written entirely by Captain Shields, outlined the 1976 Iran Incident. On many occasions within the record, he copied verbatim the details from the original DIA report. So could his introduction, where he stated that the report would be "filed away and probably forgotten," have motivated a "Secret" classification stamp? The mere fact that this U.S. Air Force captain went on the record with such a strong statement, having come from the same agency that concluded UFOs were not a threat to national security, is a big deal. This particular case shows they are absolutely a threat. And Captain Shields went on the record stating he believed it was all going to be filed away and ignored. For decades, he was absolutely right.

Other records were released, which included Department of State Airgrams sent throughout the Project Blue Book era, but let's face it, the pièce de résistance would definitely have been the hundreds of withheld COMINT reports that the NSA would not release. Those were still classified when my fight began, and the NSA would not let go of a single page.

It took years and multiple FOIA requests to get the NSA to consider their release. I know I was not the only one requesting the information, but I will say that I was fighting extremely hard for them to do it. Finally, after years of requesting, the NSA began to review the COMINT records for release.

I will admit I was quite excited to see that these records would finally be released. It was a huge fight and ultimately a triumph for everyone who took part. I remember receiving the package for the first time and opening it up because I knew that this would be it—the end to a long fight that ended with a huge victory in the pursuit of the truth! At least, that was my thought as I was tearing open that package.

I realized the moment I pulled the records out of the envelope that there was a huge problem. The majority of the records were fully redacted, and they were heavily blacked out and even whited out to lessen the striking visual appearance of "blacked-out" information. The documents were still considered classified "Top Secret," which is why the majority of them were all redacted. In fact, some pages literally only had a few words that were readable; the rest was redacted or not released at all. Although I was still excited to see them, I often wonder why they cut down those poor trees to photocopy hundreds of pages of redacted material where you can't really read anything at all. But alas, I fought for them and now I got them. Now what?

The fact that the documents were still classified "Top Secret" is in itself a huge revelation on how sensitive these UFO documents remained. It also taught me that the NSA had not lost interest in the topic one bit. It remained classified at the highest level, and even after pushing for years (and we can even safely say decades since the original CAUS court case), the NSA would not budge when it came to releasing the majority of the material.

These records do tell a story, despite the lack of detailed information. The fact that they are dated well after 1969, the close of Project Blue Book, and the fact that are still considered "Top Secret" speaks volumes about how important they are.

Nearly every reference to "UFOs" that you *can read* in these heavily redacted documents is followed by the parenthetical "(probably a balloon)." I bring this up because it clearly shows how seemingly dismissive the NSA reports were to these UFO cases, despite not a single true investigation ever being done on them. So what is that about? If there is nothing to the topic about UFOs, then

CATEGORY = 405   M =   10

MESSAGE = P171P624

18P214111B1"1111764 #2135 ANNNVZ11CZCCLLS311CFC186
PP   CE

ZNY MMCRN
ZKZK PP   CE

ZEM   KCFCRN

Figure 10.4. Single-page COMINT report clearly showing that the "Top Secret" information is still withheld from the public.

why collect the intelligence at all? If there is something to the intelligence, then why dismiss it all as a balloon and waste taxpayer money? One of those statements seems to be the truth behind it all, yet neither one makes any sense.

With all of that said, there is one amazing part of this saga with the NSA that I will close this chapter with. There is a part of the FOIA that is rarely used by researchers, but it is our right to use when we want. It is called a "Mandatory

Declassification Review," or MDR request. This came to be after the 1995 sign-ing of Executive Order 12958 by President Bill Clinton.

The FOIA stipulates that if you ask for a document, they need to give it to you if the information does not fall within the nine FOIA exemption categories. An MDR request is a bit different. MDR requests are filed to ask for a review of documents if they contain "national security" information. There are many technical differences, and those differences truly are a book in itself, but I will talk briefly about my interpretation of the difference and how I use MDRs dif-ferently than FOIA requests.

When I seek information, I generally use the FOIA. For example, I will request everything pertaining to a project name or contract number or many other examples. The FOIA officers receive my request and process it. An MDR is generally used for making an agency review or re-review a record they may have previously released (or previously denied).

Again, there are many differences here on a legal and overall technical nature, but an MDR is critical to getting information reviewed for release. During the course of a FOIA request, let's say for "Project X," all documents are rounded up and reviewed for a release. In this example, I will say that the request was filed in the year 2000 and the requester received five hundred pages of material pertaining to that request. However, many of the pages were blacked out as they were still classified.

Now let's say another researcher comes along in 2010 and files an identical request for all files on "Project X." Generally, the agency can look back, see the information has been released in part before, and will send that batch of partially blacked-out records that were released in 2000. Case closed.

Can you catch what is wrong with that scenario? There is no second review on most cases. The agency will continue to send out the same files as reviewed in 2000 for years and even a decade or decades beyond the original request. The issue I have with this is what is classified in 2000 is not necessarily clas-sified in 2010. Therefore you *should* conduct another review for the 2010 request, but sadly, agencies don't normally do that.

An MDR request can fix that for you. Instead of filing a FOIA request for the material, you can file an MDR and request that the responsive records are reviewed for possible release. I have done this many times before to get records re-reviewed and am happy to say the process works, and in many cases I was able to get the redacted portions later released.

That is the nutshell version of what the differences are, but I decided to make MDR requests work for me, especially with UFO-related requests like mine with the NSA. These UFO records that the NSA has released, and those that have been withheld in full, have largely been sent out in the same manner for literally decades. The NSA will actually keep sending out the same documents that were originally blacked out in the 1980s and 1990s to every requester that asks for them but never conduct another review—that is, until it is requested in an MDR.

On July 24, 2013, I filed an MDR request to the NSA to have them look over all the previously released UFO records and see what, if any, blacked-out markings they could remove. It took nearly one full year to process, and on July 21, 2014, the NSA sent me a response.

They stated:

> This responds to your request of 24 July 2013 to have previously released and redacted classified records pertaining to Unidentified Flying Objects (UFOs) currently posted on the Internet at URL http://www.nsa.gov/public info/declass/ ufo/index.shtml reviewed for declassification. With the exception of the enclosed document, we cannot locate unredacted copies or the original documents that were previously reviewed and released to the public.

They lost them? *All* of them but one? How likely do you think that really is? Let's interpret this statement. When the NSA first reviewed these COMINT reports to be released, they did so in the mid- to late 1990s and reviewed the unredacted copies. They made a set of blacked-out/whited-out records to release and somehow misplaced/shredded/lost all of the originals.

That may not be surprising to some with the track record of the U.S. government's organizational skills, but from the viewpoint of someone who utilizes the FOIA, I would say that is not too common. Generally, these agencies will have multiple copies, in paper form and/or digital form, of every record they have in their original state. Yet we are supposed to believe that the NSA somehow lost or destroyed some of the most sought-after UFO records to date.

What they were able to find, which I received, was another copy of the "Top Secret" Yeates affidavit. This version had less black than any other version released before it but still covered up the true nature of *why* the NSA will not let loose their UFO information.

Not that any of it matters now, but let's just say the NSA finally got to a point where they felt there would be no threat to national security if they released the contents of those COMINT reports. What would happen? We would learn nothing because in 2014, the NSA began claiming they lost 100 percent of those reports.

NATIONAL SECURITY AGENCY
CENTRAL SECURITY SERVICE
FORT GEORGE G. MEADE, MARYLAND 20755-6000

Serial: MDR-73494
21 July 2014

Mr. John Greenewald

Dear Mr. Greenewald:

This responds to your request of 24 July 2013 to have previously released and redacted classified records pertaining to Unidentified Flying Objects (UFOs) currently posted on the Internet at URL http://www.nsa.gov/public info/declass/ufo/index.shtml reviewed for declassification. With the exception of the enclosed document, we cannot locate unredacted copies or the original documents that were previously reviewed and released to the public.

The one document we were able to locate has been reviewed under the Mandatory Declassification Review (MDR) requirements of Executive Order (E.O.) 13526 and is enclosed. We have determined that some of the information in the material continues to require protection. Portions redacted from the document were found to be currently and properly classified in accordance with E.O. 13526. The redacted information meets the criteria for classification as set forth in Section 1.4 subparagraphs (b), (c), and (d) and remains classified TOP SECRET as provided in Section 1.2 of E.O. 13526. The withheld information is exempt from automatic declassification in accordance with Section 3.3(b)(3) and (6) of the Executive Order. In addition, Section 3.5(c) of E.O. 13526 allows for the protection afforded to information under the provisions of law. Therefore, information that would reveal NSA/CSS functions and activities has been protected in accordance with Section 6, Public Law 86-36 (50 U.S. Code 3605, formerly 50 U.S. Code 402 note). You may consider this a denial of your request for declassification of the above referenced document. You may also consider NSA's inability to locate the other requested records a denial of your request.

Figure 10.5. Letter sent to me on July 21, 2014, informing me they "cannot locate" all of the UFO-related documents, with the exception of the Yeates affidavit.

Although this history is lost forever, thankfully, not all agencies fell down the path of destroying their original copies of UFO records or lying about their existence. Intelligence agencies throughout the United States have sent me their records—and I am happy to say the information within only made this UFO mystery even more intriguing and even more of a threat that needs addressing.

11

UFOS AND THE CIA

Thus far, we have only explored a select few intelligence agencies, and already I feel you can deduce that the UFO connection with the U.S government stretches far beyond what they want us to believe. However, tackling the Central Intelligence Agency (CIA) adds another batch of documents into the evidence pool—and yet again we can prove that the UFO connection goes much deeper than an easily explained conventional phenomenon.

Just like the NSA, the CIA was one of my first targets when I began using the FOIA, and the battle with them to get their UFO records released would take years to achieve.

Their history was complicated yet simple when it came to the release of UFO information. Back in 1996/1997, when I was fighting for the CIA to release their records, they sent me a bill to purchase approximately nine hundred pages of material. This batch of records consisted of UFO information that spanned from the beginning years of the CIA in 1947 through approximately 1980. The release of this batch of records is much more unclear than the NSA court case, but I do know that in 1978, attorney Peter Gersten sued the CIA under Civil Action No. 78-859 for the release of this particular set of UFO records. He scored a victory when he received this nine-hundred-plus-page cache of material, and it has been disseminated by the CIA to all who ask for them ever since. Of course, you just had to pay for them.

However, I was not interested in the records that had already been released. Why? Well, researchers had scrutinized them to death, and I wanted the material that had yet to be released. This unveiled, in my opinion, a rather shady game that the CIA was playing with me. They were not very open with FOIA requesters like myself, stating that they stopped adding to this collection for purchase but rather continued to sell a "dated" collection of material that I believed was not complete. I knew that the records in this package for sale ended circa 1980—so my biggest question was: where is the recent material?

In 1996/1997, there was approximately more than a decade and a half of possible UFO records to be released, but I was not sure if *any* even existed. Call it a hunch, but I assumed since most agencies and military branches did not stop collecting UFO intelligence after Project Blue Book, the CIA did not stop after this civil action by Mr. Gersten. So therefore, I knew there had to be more.

What I was not prepared for was the fight that the CIA was going to give about these more recent UFO records. In fact, I had to go back and forth multiple times before the CIA even acknowledged I was asking for the UFO records post 1980. Even though I spelled it out clearly in my request, I was always met with a bill to purchase the nine hundred pages they had released to Mr. Gersten in 1980. They would never mention what I actually asked for, which was documents beyond that date.

After literally more than a couple of years going back and forth, the CIA officially acknowledged I was seeking UFO records post 1980, and in response, they sent me another bill. This was during the course of processing FOIA Request F-1999-02173. The CIA was charging hundreds of dollars to purchase a couple thousand pages of additional UFO documents. So now I was finally going to get what I was looking for; I just had to find the money to get it.

I was still in high school at this time. In fact, this was senior year, and I was about to graduate and move on to college. I did not have a huge paying job at this point, so the combined total of being approximately $450 at the time was a lot of money to me. However, through my own pocket change and some gracious donations that were sent in to me by those who believed in what I was doing, I raised the money and purchased *both* collections of documents.

According to the CIA, this purchase would give me everything they had on UFOs, a couple thousand pages of which had never seen the light of day. When I received the boxes of records in the mail, I was incredibly excited. It was not easy for me to save that much money at the time, and a fight that lasted a couple years was at an end. The documents were finally right in front of me after all those years fighting for them.

The first of the boxes was the 990-plus pages that were released to Mr. Gersten in the civil action in 1979. Although interesting, I thumbed through them to find what you would expect—1950s and 1960s typewritten UFO reports from around the globe. Some were blacked out and redacted, while others seemed to be unclassified. But let's face it—it was that second box that was worth more than I could explain.

I recall ripping open the box, and there they were. I was face to face with thousands of pages of UFO records that I was about to touch—never before reaching any hands outside of the CIA itself. At this time, I used to use red pencils to mark the back of each page—in case I were to drop a stack of hundreds of pages, I knew which order they came in, and I could put them back together.

With a pencil in hand, I began going through page by page to number them, and while doing so, I noticed something really bizarre and disheartening. Unlike the first box, of those typewritten pages that just had a certain look and feel to them, these were "clean" and they all looked the same. I quickly realized that I had just paid hundreds of dollars for a stack of thousands of pages of newspaper articles from around the globe that were retyped into clean, computer-printed pieces of paper.

Yes, that's right; all of them were the text of newspaper articles collected by the Foreign Broadcast Information Service, or FBIS. This program began as the Foreign Broadcast Monitoring Service (FBMS) by President Franklin D. Roosevelt in 1941. After the bombing of Pearl Harbor, the name was changed to the Foreign Broadcast Intelligence Service (FBIS); the program was later renamed the Foreign Broadcast Information Service (FBIS) and transferred to the CIA.

The mission was simple: monitor foreign broadcasts on television, radio, and print and archive pertinent material for intelligence reasons. It is known that the FBIS did not collect all the broadcasts by foreign entities throughout the globe, but rather material that could be valuable to the U.S. intelligence communities.

This second box contained only material from FBIS. So therefore, the information came from Russian newspapers like *Pravda* and even monitored the television programs that aired throughout the globe. As a result of newspapers such as these, along with broadcasts on television, if the acronym "UFO" came up, the document was printed and sent to me, after I paid for it.

I do not want to say it was a total waste of money, but it was not what I was expecting. Newspapers are public source documents, so why would I want to pay for them from the CIA? In addition, why was there such a fight to get the CIA to even release them in the first place? I have a theory to that, and I hope I am wrong.

When Mr. Gersten got the 990-plus pages released in 1980, as I mentioned earlier, it consisted of what we would expect: those typewritten, and in some cases handwritten, documents about UFOs; the intelligence gathered and data viable to unraveling the mystery of the phenomenon like location, speed, altitude, and so on. Yet what are the astronomical odds (pardon the pun) that Mr. Gersten came along, created his civil action, got 990-plus pages released, and that just happened to be the exact year that the CIA said to themselves, "Yeah, let's just not collect UFO information anymore and just focus on UFO-related newspaper articles"? Those odds would be so beyond extraordinary that we could easily dismiss that possibility.

What is more likely is I probably annoyed the heck out of the CIA FOIA officers, and they were not used to people asking questions and pursuing documents that the CIA did not want to talk about. Mr. Gersten made a great stride getting those records released, and they told an amazing story. The CIA probably did not want to allow me the opportunity to do that again with records from the 1990s. So, therefore, in order to shut me up, they concocted the idea to just go to the FBIS, enter the search term "UFO"—and charge for everything they spit out of that database.

How do I know they probably just did that and that only? Because every occurrence of the acronym "UFO" in these newly released documents was bold. To anyone with any computer search-term experience, normally when you do a text-based search, the results will have your search term bolded or, in more recent years, highlighted.

I am not sure if the CIA just expected my teenage self to not be able to pay for the documents, or if they did not even care I would put the pieces together to show their scam just to shut me up, but alas, here I was having paid for thousands of pages of newspaper articles.

Let me back up a bit and talk about the documents themselves, now that you know about the fight it took to get them released. First, I will deal with the first batch of records that I opened, which consisted of records dated 1980 and prior. In this batch, there are a large number of records from the Project Blue Book era, which is no surprise. However, on the top of the stack was one of the rare cases during the Project Blue Book era wherein a report was classified. As I mentioned earlier about Project Blue Book, the majority of material was considered "unclassified" and was largely open to reporters during the 1960s and beyond, should they ask to see them. In the years that followed, the public had unfiltered access, as well. However, this was an exception and detailed a case from September 21, 1957. The document formerly classified as "Secret" read the following:

1. As reported by components of the US Air Defense Command, an unidentified flying object (UFO) was tracked by US radars on a relatively straight course from the eastern tip of Long Island to the vicinity of Buffalo. The object was reportedly moving westward at an altitude of 50,000 feet and speed of 2,000

kts. "Jamming" was reported by several radars in this vicinity and westward as far as Chicago. In a subsequent briefing for representatives of the IAC, the US Air Force reported that the original reports had been degraded somewhat by information that: (a) there was an 11 minute break in the tracks; (b) weather conditions in the area were of the type which have in the past produced false radar pips and electronic interference; (c) B-47's of SAC were in the area near Chicago on an ECM training flight. The ADC has not completed its investigation of this incident, but in any event it now seems clear that the phenomena reported west of Buffalo were not related to the UFO.

2. We have no intelligence on Soviet activities (e.g., long-range air, submarine, or merchant shipping operations) which can be related specifically to this reported event. We believe it unlikely that a Soviet aircraft could conduct a mission at this speed and altitude and return to Bloc territory. However, we credit the USSR with the capability to have a submarine-launched cruise-type missile of low subsonic [supersonic] performance and a range of about 500 n.m., but we have no specific evidence of the existence of such a missile.

3. We have examined possible Soviet motives for launching a one-way vehicle on an operation over the US, and consider that there would be little motivation at this time, except possibly a psychological or retaliatory motive, which we believe is marginal. One-way reconnaissance operations are largely ruled out by the likelihood that the results would be of small value, and the risk of compromise would be very great.

4. We conclude, therefore, that it is highly improbable that a Soviet operation is responsible for the UFO reports of 20 September.

5. Considering the fact that the ADC investigation is incomplete, and that weather phenomena are increasingly likely explanations of the original reports, we recommend that no IAC meeting be called on this subject at this time.

At the bottom of the document was the distribution list of all agencies that received this UFO briefing document. This included the Atomic Energy Commission (AEC) (now known as the Department of Energy), Office of Naval Intelligence (ONI), Federal Bureau of Investigation (FBI), Joint Intelligence Group (JIG), Department of the Army, Department of the Air Force, Department of State and, of course, the CIA.

I tracked down what I believe is the subsequent report and investigation in the Project Blue Book files. The folder contained what appears to be a total of fifty-two pages and was also formerly classified "Secret." Whenever a classification like this exists in a program that is supposedly considered "Unclassified," the question then becomes: why? What is on this record that makes it get a higher classification than most reports during the Project Blue Book era?

At 1916Z, Benton received four overlap pre-plots from 26th AD Control Center on an unidentified target said to be heading west at 2,000 knots with an estimated altitude of 50,000 feet. At 1917Z Benton detected a target on the vertical upper beam heading northwest with an estimated speed of 920 knots. This target was correlated as being BB-6 from Montauk. The track was carried on VU until contact was lost at a point approximately 135 n.mi. northwest of the station. It was again picked up on vertical center and tracked until it faded at 1926Z. No further pickup on this track was made.

At 1924Z the second track was detected on VU 75 n.mi. north of the station heading 290°, estimated speed 1,200 knots. This track had no correlation and was numbered BE-111. It was carried on VU until contact was lost at a point approximately 145 n.mi. northwest of the station. It was again picked up on vertical center at 160 n.mi. northwest and carried until it faded at 190 n.mi., 305°. Both tracks were interrogated by Mark X with no response. All track information was passed to the ACW site at Lockport and Claysburg but these sites did not detect either of these tracks. Lockport was off the air for maintenance during the entire time Benton was tracking and did not return to operation until 1935Z, one minute after the track BE-111 faded. Lockport observed the residual effects of the chaff drop. Anti-aircraft units in the area of concern did not report any unusual, high-speed target activity.

B-58 aircraft activity was considered as a possible cause for the track at Benton AFS; however, a message to WADC established that no B-58s were flying in this area at this time.

Figure 11.1. This page confirms the track was at 50,000 feet traveling 2,000 knots, or 2,301 mph.

Let's briefly dissect it. In paragraph 1, it is stated that a UFO was tracked at 50,000 feet going 2,000 knots. This is converted to more than 2,301 mph. Keep in mind this was 1957, and according to the *Guinness Book of World Records*, the fastest aircraft at the time was a McDonnell F-101A "Voodoo," which was clocked at going 1,200–1,300 mph on December of 1957 at Edwards Air Force Base. This record was made about two months after the UFO event, so what could this unknown object be in September of the same year traveling nearly twice the speed?

In fact, the UFO's reported speed was so great that Guinness would not actually have the 2,100 mph record broken until nearly twenty years later, as achieved by the SR-71 Blackbird, also at Edwards Air Force Base, on July 28, 1976. Even with that flight, it still was not quite at the 2,300-plus mph speed of the UFO in this document. So what could this be?

The biggest concern by the intelligence community at this time was that it had a Soviet origin. They feared it could be a reconnaissance aircraft, missile, or some other show of technological strength, though the document went on to discount that. The CIA document dismissed any Soviet connection to the event.

Paragraph 1 also talked about jamming of multiple radar stations, but then tried to discount the entire event as being related to the weather. The weather? This is where these classification stamps play a crucial role in determining a document's value. If this was all an illusion, caused by a weather phenomenon, what is so classified about that? There are countless reports from the Project Blue Book era in the archives that are "explained" cases where weather is to blame, and those reports are "Unclassified" and they never received a classification higher than that. However, this record, with potentially the same explanation, held a "Secret" designation when it was written.

We can discount the theory that this was simply a CIA action to classify the case, and when Project Blue Book got a hold of it, they dropped it to "Unclassified." Why can we discount that theory? The fifty-two-page folder of records within Project Blue Book held the same "Secret" classification. In other words, something about this case was truly classified.

Since paragraphs 2–4 only discredit a Soviet connection, then paragraph 5 attempts to blame the weather, it seems likely that the cause of the "Secret" stamp was due to the UFO's technical capabilities. It should be noted that the U.S. Air Force dismissed the entire case as being equipment malfunction and nothing more. Then why keep the report "Secret," which was contradictory to most of the UFO reports they collected?

Beyond the Project Blue Book era, the CIA documents continued to chronicle UFO cases and encounters. What was very evident with this batch of material is that the CIA was still actively collecting UFO intelligence reports from around the globe. This fact, yet again, contradicts that "company line" having been said years prior that the U.S. government held no interest in this phenomenon.

A visually striking document came in the form of a three-page record wherein nearly everything of substance was blacked out and redacted. You can see it was dated May 8, 1975, and concerned the former Soviet Union. However, that is all the information that can be gathered from the first page. The rest of it is entirely blacked out and redacted. The second page held an incredibly hard-to-read but discernible two-line statement, which read, "Deny in toto," and the second line is believed to read, "1 page." In other words, "in toto" is Latin for "completely" or "in total"—so the CIA will not release anything on the page and will save their black ink instead of redacting it all. This clearly continues to show how secretive and sensitive the UFO topic is within the intelligence community.

Another document I will highlight is from February 9, 1978, and is in the form of a memorandum with the subject line "Report of a UFO at Time of Soviet Satellite Failure." The body of the memorandum read the following:

1. At 4:30 on 8 February 1978, [REDACTED], who works for the [RE-DACTED], reported information that might relate to the Soviet satellite that fell in Canada on Tuesday, 24 January. He said that while going to work a week ago Friday, 27 January, he was on the bridge in [REDACTED] going over towards [REDACTED] and he observed an odd object coming down in the sky. No description was obtained.
2. We said we would pass his information to the Air Force, and if they wanted to contact him for more information we would give the Air Force his name and telephone number.
3. For the record, in the event that anyone is tracking UFOs, we forward the following:
   [REDACTED] [REDACTED] [REDACTED] [REDACTED]

The biggest question here, other than why UFO intelligence was still being collected in 1978, dealt with why the information would be passed to the Air Force. Nine years prior to this event, the Air Force stated they did not want UFO information anymore—from the public or otherwise. The mystery was solved, yet the CIA was collecting UFO-related evidence and forwarding it to them. What is even more intriguing about this document is in paragraph 3, wherein the memo stated, "For the record, in the event that anyone is tracking

TITLE:

CCCREFERENCE: GO332111S2375,
08MAY75, 2PP
USSF

INFCDATE: 594,

APPROVED FOR RELEASE
Date 19 May 69

19.

Figure 11.2.   Example of a heavily classified Central Intelligence Agency (CIA) UFO document.

UFOs, we forward the following:" and then the next line is completely redacted. What could be on this line that needs to be withheld?

The CIA records were continuing to paint the picture that whatever the real story was behind the UFO phenomenon, it was not solved, and it was still heavily classified. With only a few records highlighted here, we can drive home yet again the points that UFOs were real; the U.S. government did not stop collecting intelligence relating to them in 1969; the topic was classified on many levels; and finally, whatever the phenomenon really was, they had no explanation for it.

This was somewhat reinforced by the second release to me of UFO-related documents, dated from 1980 through approximately 1997, from the CIA. This was the release that consisted entirely of newspaper articles.

Although incredibly disappointing, especially after seeing my examples above at the caliber of UFO intelligence the CIA had collected from the 1950s through the 1970s, it really reinforced the interest the CIA had in the phenomenon. Despite my disappointment, the stack of newspaper article text proved to me that the CIA was still collecting UFO information on some level. I can only guess, and I stress it is a guess, that the CIA has more than this from 1980 on relating to UFOs. Common sense tells me that the court case by Mr. Gersten did not coincidentally fall on the same date they transitioned to just collecting newspaper articles. Be that as it may, as an investigator, I can only use the evidence that is in front of me.

With these records, we can deduce that the CIA still collected UFO intelligence in the form of newspaper articles and the text within them. From an intelligence standpoint, this is the cheapest way to "keep tabs" on the topic, without having millions of dollars "on the books" for UFO research. Instead, they could hide their interest within the funding of the FBIS. When people audited spending records, UFOs would not be a line item, but the FBIS would and that would not be a cause for alarm or question.

The FBIS consisted of collecting newspaper articles on a long list of topics, not just UFOs, so no one would place that connection. Until, of course, someone screamed to the high heavens under the FOIA to get their UFO documents post 1980 released. So I seemingly exposed that tactic of collecting UFO information. Oops.

Fast forward to 1997 and the CIA published an article by the National Reconnaissance Office (NRO) historian Gerald K. Haines in the CIA's "Studies in Intelligence" internal newsletter. In this particular "Unclassified" article, Mr. Haines stated:

> In November 1954, CIA had entered into the world of high technology with its
> U-2 overhead reconnaissance project. Working with Lockheed's Advanced De-

velopment facility in Burbank, California, known as the Skunk Works, and Kelly Johnson, an eminent aeronautical engineer, the Agency by August 1955 was testing a high-altitude experimental aircraft—the U-2. It could fly at 60,000 feet; in the mid-1950s, most commercial airliners flew between 10,000 feet and 20,000 feet. Consequently, once the U-2 started test flights, commercial pilots and air traffic controllers began reporting a large increase in UFO sightings.

The early U-2s were silver (they were later painted black) and reflected the rays from the sun, especially at sunrise and sunset. They often appeared as fiery objects to observers below. Air Force BLUE BOOK investigators aware of the secret U-2 flights tried to explain away such sightings by linking them to natural phenomena such as ice crystals and temperature inversions. By checking with the Agency's U-2 Project Staff in Washington, BLUE BOOK investigators were able to attribute many UFO sightings to U-2 flights. They were careful, however, not to reveal the true cause of the sighting to the public.

In 2011, a declassified report originally designated "Secret" was released in part to the public. It was titled "The Central Intelligence Agency and Overhead Reconnaissance: The U-2 and OXCART Programs, 1954–1974." In this report, it also reinforced that the CIA was trying to "take credit" for the UFO sightings that spanned decades. They believed that the majority of UFO reports were actually sightings of various U-2 flights, and although Project Blue Book officers knew the U-2 was to blame for many UFO-related events, they were part of the cover-up to that program's existence. Project Blue Book investigators could not reveal the sensitive nature of the U-2 program and therefore did not label UFO cases accurately. At least, that's what the CIA wanted us to believe.

Finally, on July 2, 2014, a fairly controversial CIA tweet was posted on Twitter that showed the CIA was putting all their faith in this theory. The tweet read:

Remember reports of unusual activity in the skies in the '50s? That was us. #U2Week #UFODAY

The tweet then linked to the report I just mentioned.

That is a fairly bold statement to make, don't you think? I mean, everything that happened in the 1950s was the CIA's U-2 program? It seems so straightforward and written with such confidence, I would bet money that most people would believe such a statement in the form of a tweet and then discount UFO reports all together. I would even guess that was their intent from the start.

That is, it may be believable until you want to apply some logic and common sense. Let's deal only with the CIA documents to see if we can prove, or disprove, this outstanding tweet. First, let's go back to that case from 1957, wherein the document attempted to dismiss it away as a weather event. Despite that explanation, a UFO was seen, crossing multiple states, jamming radars along the way, and traveling at more than 2,300 mph and an elevation of 50,000 feet.

The U-2's top speed is 500 mph or Mach .67 (that's point 67). That is a far cry from taking credit for a 2,300 mph aircraft. Although the U-2 could fly at a reported 70,000 feet in the air, and that in itself matches the 50,000-foot altitude of the UFO, you would still not be anywhere near the speed to be the cause of it—therefore, we can easily dismiss that label.

In addition to juxtaposing this document to the U-2's capabilities, let's also know that the first flight of the U-2 was on August 1, 1955. That is more than halfway through the decade of the 1950s, yet the CIA claims their craft takes credit for everything. None of that makes any sense because according to Project Blue Book statistics, there were at least 339 cases in the first half of the 1950s that were considered "unknown." Certainly, the CIA is not trying to rewrite history or claim the U-2 also has time-travel capabilities, right?

The CIA has a long history on UFOs, but what deepens this mystery is their attempt to jump into the game in 2014 and try to essentially "take credit" for being the cause of the sightings. They then double down on that claim, stating that the entire 1950s decade of UFO events was caused by their aircraft that only began flying in 1955.

Under the FOIA, I went after documents relating to this tweet. Yes, under the FOIA, you can go after e-mails and internal memos that you may not think even exist, but when a CIA tweet is released, someone with access just does not make the lone decision to tweet it out. Tweets and press releases and whatever the CIA decides to disseminate to the public have a decision-making process. In fact, there are social media strategy handbooks created by most agencies that outline what types of posts should or should not appear under their respective social network accounts.

The CIA is no different, so I wanted to take a sneak peek at what their line of reasoning was for this particular statement. My request asked for the following:

1. All e-mails, memos, letters, correspondence, etc. relating to the creation of this tweet. This would include, but not be limited to, the social network teams, web programmers, writers, and all CIA personnel involved in this tweet.
2. All documents compiled to research and fact-check for this tweet.

It took more a year to get a single page released by the CIA that pertained to the above. It gave an inside look at how much thought went into the tweet.

From: _____   (b)(3)
Sent: Wednesday, July 02, 2014 2:43 PM
To: _____   (b)(3)
Cc: _____   (b)(3)
Subject: RE: Today is #UFODay

Classification: UNCLASSIFIED
==

I love it. Good to go

From: _____   (b)(3)
Sent: Wednesday, July 02, 2014 2:39 PM
To: _____   (b)(3)
Cc: _____   (b)(3)
Subject: Today is #UFODay

Classification: UNCLASSIFIED
==

I am almost afraid to bring it up, but it is apparently World UFO Day, who know?

We could tie it into U2 Week!

Reports of unusual activity in the sky in the '50s? That was just us. #U2Week #UFODay
Link to the U-2 doc and photo of excerpt – attached.

I use that line in my tours, it always goes over well.

_____   (b)(3)
CIA.gov
_____   (b)(3)

==
Classification: UNCLASSIFIED
==
Classification: UNCLASSIFIED

Figure 11.3. E-mails regarding the CIA's UFO tweet indicate that it was very much rushed and not researched.

The single page was a succession of two e-mails, sent to and from unknown individuals, as the names are redacted due to a CIA statute protecting their identities. The first e-mail was sent presumably to a boss or someone at a higher position with the agency that read:

"I am almost afraid to bring it up, but it is apparently World UFO Day, who know [sic]?

We could tie it into U2 Week!
Reports of unusual activity in the sky in the '50s? That was just us. #U2Week
#UFODay
Link to the U-2 doc and photo of excerpt—attached.
I use that line in my tours, it always goes over well.

The response from the recipient of the above was short and sweet. Whomever this e-mail went to, he or she simply replied with the following:

I love it. Good to go

The response was so rushed; they forgot an end period on their e-mail. The first e-mail was so rushed, they didn't even use proper grammar. Although I tend to not judge and go into "Grammar Nazi" mode, it is fairly indicative of the amount of thought that went into this blast to their followers. Not only was it inaccurate, it was downright misleading and lacked any thought or research.

Recall my specific request that I provided a few paragraphs before this. I asked for all documents and e-mails that would show the fact checking and entirely who was involved and at what levels research was even done. You would think, with such a bold statement by the CIA and then my request, it would all yield more than a single page relating to what I asked for. Yet, there was just this one single page of two e-mails. It clearly showed no thought, no research, and no fact checking.

As these intelligence agencies continued to pile on the reports, and they released them to me under the FOIA, I knew there had to be some kind of protocol to it all, some kind of method to the madness. After researching many topics, I learned that there are policies, procedures, and protocols for nearly everything. There are procedures for writing procedures and protocols to writing protocols. So my next quest led to how the post–Project Blue Book documents came to be. Was there policy, procedure, or protocol for reporting these things?

Not only was my hunch right that something like this would exist—but the U.S. government tried to pull a magic trick to make it all go away after I made an amazing discovery.

UFO REGULATIONS THAT SHOULD AND SHOULD NOT EXIST

As the top intelligence agencies have proven quite a bit when it comes to UFOs, I want to switch gears in this chapter to speak to how those UFO records came to be. The sheer existence of these documents proves a story and discredits the overall narrative that the U.S. government and military want us to believe about the topic.

However, the bigger question I had in my mind as I was receiving these thousands of pages was how the documents came to be in the first place. Recall previously that I stated that there are protocols to writing protocols and manuals to writing manuals, so I knew deep down that there had to be a root to these UFO records. Memorandums, intelligence reports, letters, and so on just do not appear out of thin air for no reason or without direction. So the question is: what was that method?

During the Project Blue Book era, the U.S. Air Force wanted to have certain types of information when they received a UFO sighting. So, in order to meet that need, they wrote certain regulations to follow when handling a UFO report. Air Force Regulation 200-2 was first established August 23, 1953, and although there were many revisions of the record through to the end of Project Blue Book, the gist of it remained the same. According to one version of Air Force Regulation 200-2:

> This regulation establishes the UFO Program to investigate and analyze UFO's over the United States. Such investigation and analysis are directly related to Air Force responsibility for the defense of the United States. The UFO program provides for the prompt reporting and rapid reporting needed for successful "identification," which is the second of four phases of air defense—detection,

identification, interception and destruction. All commanders will comply strictly with this regulation.

This regulation then spelled out exactly what to report and how to report it. However, it is one excerpt that truly shows, in my opinion, the nail in the coffin (as if you needed another) that Project Blue Book was not a true investigation but rather an effort at an explanation to reduce public interest in the phenomenon.

Reduction of Percentage of UFO "Unidentifieds" Air Force activities must reduce the percentage of unidentified to the minimum. Analysis thus far has explained all but a few of the sightings reported. These unexplained sightings are carried statistically as unidentifieds.

This paragraph solidifies that there was nothing scientific about Project Blue Book from the start. A true scientific study would never come out of the starting gate with an effort to reduce statistics on anything. This negates the whole scientific process in the first place. Statistics should be driven by true and tested results, rather than tests aimed at reducing (or increasing) any given number. That is a flawed approach.

That aside, the regulation did outline a detailed list of characteristics that should accompany any report that came in. This is spelled out in great detail:

d. Report Format Reports will include the following numbered items:
(1) Description of the object(s):
(a) Shape.
(b) Size compared to known object (use one of the following terms: Head of a pin, pea, dime, nickel, quarter, half dollar, silver dollar, baseball, grapefruit, or basketball) held in the hand at about arms length.
(c) Color.
(d) Number.
(e) Formation, if more than one.
(f) Any discernible features or details.
(g) Tail, trail, or exhaust, including size of same compared to size of object(s).
(h) Sound. If heard, describe sound.
(i) Other pertinent or unusual features.
(2) Description of course of object(s):
(a) What first called the attention of the observer(s) to the object(s)?
(b) Angle of elevation and azimuth of the objects when first observed.
(c) Angle of elevation and azimuth of the objects upon disappearance.
(d) Description of flight path and maneuvers of object(s).
(e) Manner of disappearance of objects(s).

(f) Length of time in sight.

(3) Manner of observation:

(a) Use one or a combination of the following items: Ground-visual, ground-electronic, air-electronic. (If electronic, specify type of radar.)

(b) Statement as to optical aids (telescopes, binoculars, and so forth) used and description thereof.

(c) If the sighting is made while airborne, give type of aircraft, identification number, altitude, heading, speed, and home station.

(4) Time and date of sighting:

(a) Zulu time-date group of sighting.

(b) Light conditions (use one of the following terms): Night, day, dawn, dusk.

(5) Locations of observer(s). Exact latitude and longitude of each observer or Georef position, or position with reference to a known landmark.

(6) Identifying information of all observer(s):

(a) Civilian—Name, age, mailing address, occupation.

(b) Military—Name, grade, organization, duty, and estimate of reliability.

(7) Weather and winds-aloft conditions at time and place of sightings:

(a) Observer(s) account of weather conditions.

(b) Report from nearest AWS or U.S. Weather Bureau Office of wind direction and velocity in degrees and knots at surface, 6,000', 10,000', 16,000', 20,000', 30,000', 50,000', and 80,000', if available.

(c) Ceiling.

(d) Visibility.

(e) Amount of cloud cover.

(f) Thunderstorms in area and quadrant in which located.

(8) Any other unusual activity or condition, meteorological, astronomical, or otherwise, which might account for the sighting.

(9) Interception and identification action taken. (Such action may be taken whenever feasible, complying with existing air defense directives.)

(10) Location of any air traffic in the general area at the time of the sighting.

(11) Position title and comments of the preparing officer, including his preliminary analysis of the possible cause of the sighting(s).

(12) Security. Reports should be unclassified unless inclusion of data required by c and d below mandates a higher classification.

I wanted to include the entire list of details the Air Force required because in fairness, this part is actually quite good. This section is often used by present-day UFO research organizations to plan their UFO reporting forms and techniques they utilize to investigate a sighting. I would imagine that this particular section was heavily influenced by the scientific consultants on the project, namely Dr. J. Allen Hynek.

FOR OFFICIAL ~~UNCLASSIFIED~~ ONLY —

91-F01-1030
JANAP 146(E)
32 pgo.

CANADIAN - UNITED STATES COMMUNICATIONS INSTRUCTIONS FOR REPORTING VITAL INTELLIGENCE SIGHTINGS

(CIRVIS/MERINT) JANAP 146(E)

> THIS PUBLICATION CONTAINS US MILITARY INFORMATION AND RELEASE TO OTHER THAN US MILITARY AGENCIES WILL BE ON A NEED-TO-KNOW BASIS.

THE JOINT CHIEFS OF STAFF WASHINGTON, D.C., 20301

MARCH 1966

FOR OFFICIAL ~~UNCLASSIFIED~~ USE ONLY   I   A392

CHANGE NO. 2
(REVERSE BLANK)

Figure 12.1. Cover page for Joint Army Navy Air Force Publication (JANAP) 146(E).

Another manual worthy of mention was Joint Army Navy Air Force Publication (JANAP) 146. There are multiple variations of this publication, but revision "C" first was published on March 10, 1954, and revised a few times until its final version "E" published on March 31, 1966. The reason this manual varies from Air Force Regulation 200-2 is the fact that there is no mention of Project Blue Book, and it actually applied to a wider range of military branches, as indicated by the title of it. In addition, it broadened the types of objects to report and was not limited to unidentified aerial craft. JANAP 146(E) outlined the following:

201. Information to be Reported and When to Report.

a. Sightings within the scope of this chapter, as outlined in paragraphs 102b(1), (2), (6) and (7), are to be reported as follows:

(1) While airborne and from land based observers.

(a) Hostile or unidentified single aircraft or formations of aircraft which appear to be directed against the United States or Canada or their forces.

(b) Missiles.

(c) Unidentified flying objects.

(d) Hostile or unidentified submarines.

(e) Hostile or unidentified group or groups of military surface vessels.

(f) Individual surface vessels, submarines, or aircraft of unconventional design, or engaged in suspicious activity or observed in a location or on a course which may be interpreted as constituting a threat to the United States, Canada, or their forces.

(g) Any unexplained or unusual activity which may indicate a possible attack against or through Canada or the United States, including the presence of any unidentified or other suspicious ground parties in the polar region or other remote or sparsely populated areas.

2) Upon landing.

(a) Reports which for any reason could not be transmitted while airborne.

(b) Unlisted airfields or facilities, weather stations, or air navigation aids.

(c) Post landing reports (to include photographs or film if pictures were taken; see paragraph 104).

What JANAP 146(E) proved was that Project Blue Book may not have been the only place collecting or even investigating UFO reports. The publication also introduced a new acronym that, at the time, I had no idea would play a much larger role in my research. That acronym was for "Communications Instructions for Reporting Vital Intelligence Sightings," better referred to as CIRVIS (pronounced SIR-VEECE).

These CIRVIS reports, although dealing with other types of sightings as well, included unidentified flying objects. But why would the Air Force (among other agencies) need yet another publication outlining how and where to report UFOs? Air Force Regulation 200-2 spelled it all out already, yet here was another within the same time frame but with important differences.

What is interesting to note about JANAP 146(E) is that it also pertained to the Canadian military. This publication outlined not only procedures for military branches of the United States; it also applied to the Canadian military. What is also important is where the reports were sent to. Again, with no mention of Project Blue Book, there was a much longer list of recipients for these CIRVIS reports. As JANAP 146(E) explained:

a. The following activities have responsibilities as follows:

(1) CINCNORAD or 22ND NRHQ NORTH BAY will review all CIRVIS reports to ascertain that they have been addressed in accordance with paragraph

206 and forward reports to any omitted addressees in the United States and Canada, respectively. These headquarters are the normal points of contact between the two countries and are responsible for passing CIRVIS reports of interest, including post-landing reports, to each other.

(2) United States or Canadian military or diplomatic authorities in receipt of CIRVIS reports that have not been previously forwarded should take the action indicated in paragraph 206 without delay by the most rapid means available.

(3) Chief of Staff, USAF, will disseminate CIRVIS reports to appropriate agencies in the Washington D.C. area.

(4) ADGHQ NORTH BAY and the Canadian Maritime Commanders will be responsible for notifying National Defence Headquarters in Ottawa concerning CIRVIS reports.

(5) Sea Frontier Commanders will be responsible for notifying the Chief of Naval Operations and appropriate Fleet Commanders concerning CIRVIS reports, and for timely notification of other sea Frontier Commanders if the location of the reported contact warrants such notification.

b. Fixed and mobile military communications facilities and military personnel having occasion to handle CIRVIS reports must lend assistance in all cases required in expediting CIRVIS reports. All civilian facilities and personnel are also urged to do so. Maximum effort must be made by all persons handling CIRVIS reports to ensure positive immediate delivery.

One thing becomes abundantly clear with these paragraphs. There were a lot of other names as recipients to these CIRVIS reports, which would, by definition, include UFOs. Where was Project Blue Book mentioned? Nowhere. Was the Air Force the central source like they were in Air Force Regulation 200-2? No. JANAP 146(E) proved yet again that Project Blue Book may not have been seeing all of the evidence, especially from agencies outside the Air Force, like the Army and the Navy. Instead of an office like Project Blue Book, the reports that dealt with UFOs ended up at the North American Aerospace Defense Command (NORAD), the agency that is responsible for watching all the threats that come from above.

NORAD defines its mission as the following:

The North American Aerospace Defense Command (NORAD) is a United States and Canada bi-national organization charged with the missions of aerospace warning and aerospace control for North America. Aerospace warning includes the detection, validation, and warning of attack against North America whether by aircraft, missiles, or space vehicles, through mutual support arrangements with other commands.

Aerospace control includes ensuring air sovereignty and air defense of the airspace of Canada and the United States. The renewal of the NORAD Agreement in May 2006 added a maritime warning mission, which entails a shared awareness and understanding of the activities conducted in U.S. and Canadian maritime approaches, maritime areas and internal waterways.

With the above, it is clear that for UFO reports to go here, there was a potential threat behind them and potentially their origin. Yes, that's obviously a stretch, but for NORAD to be on the receiving end, it showed at least some kind of connection since they evaluated the CIRVIS intelligence reports.

I filed a FOIA request way back in 1998, basing it off of JANAP 146, CIRVIS, and the reality that NORAD was on the receiving end of those specific reports. I expected a response that would give me a stack of documents, but I was unaware of one major factor to getting documents from NORAD. In their letter to me, they made it clear:

> For your information, Title 5 United States Code (U.S.C.), Section 552, the Freedom of Information Act (FOIA), is a United States (US) statute and is only applicable to US agencies as defined in Title 5 U.S.C., sections 551 and 552. NORAD is a binational command, established by Volume 33, United States Treaties (UST), page 1277, subject to control of both Canadian and US Government agencies as defined in the Act and is subsequently not subject to the US FOIA.

How convenient, right? CIRVIS reports, dealing with UFOs and potentially cases that came well after Project Blue Book, were sent to one of the very few installations on U.S. soil that was not subject to the FOIA. In this same letter dated June 16, 1998, they did give me a glimmer of hope:

> However, it is our policy under NORAD Instruction 35-17, Processing Requests for NORAD Records, to release records of information where documents or information are not security classified, FOUO and/or NORAD sensitive (with applicable exemption) and are cost efficient to provide.

Well, that was good, or so I thought. Even though the FOIA did not apply, they did make an effort to comply with such requests, under this NORAD Instruction 35-17. That glimmer of hope quickly was squashed, as the next paragraph read:

> Regarding UFO/UAO phenomenon, we have no documentation, archived or otherwise, regarding this type of phenomenon and have not documented this type of information or maintained a database on same since the official closing of "Project

Blue Book" in 1969. An excellent source is the Internet, which provides a wealth of information on UFO phenomenon, past and present. Also for your information, I enclosed a UFO fact sheet that provides you with additional telephone numbers of national UFO agencies which might be able to assist you in your research.

Oh, for joy—the amazing "fact sheet" again! The pure basis for the "company line" was fed to me even from NORAD, despite the existence of JANAP 146 and the irrefutable proof that UFO reports were being generated and sent to them.

On July 10, 1998, I responded to that letter. Even though they were not subject to the FOIA, my letter served as sort of an "appeal" to further explain that JANAP 146 was "on the books" for decades in the past. And during those decades, which stretched far beyond Project Blue Book's close, it could and even should have generated UFO reports responsive to my original request. Therefore, I felt strongly, that they needed to look better and find these records I knew had to exist. All I had was another hunch at this point, but with that regulation irrefutable, I knew there had to be something.

The response came just days later in a letter NORAD sent me dated July 15, 1998. They stated in the body of their letter:

I am not familiar with the Joint Army Navy Air Force (JANAP) Publication 146(E), so perhaps you could mail or fax ((719 554-3165/4072) me the specific pages that related to NORAD and UFO report [sic] to possibly determine an Office of Primary Responsibility (OPR)?

Well, this was a new one. The same agency that told me the Internet was a great resource and I should head there, now told me they have no idea what a certain publication is and wanted me to supply it to them without ever trying to conduct an Internet search themselves? Let me not come off and sound too aggressive here because I do not mind helping agencies where I can. In fact, some agencies have FOIA staff that may be fairly inexperienced with processing requests, and I have found myself helping, assisting, or offering advice on some occasions to help them search for responsive records. I actually enjoy that and do not mind it. However, a simple Internet search even in 1998 would have come up with this record, if they really wanted to help. So for me to be forced to furnish a record that clearly stated they were the receiving end showed me I was about to enter a fight I would not win.

I grew increasingly frustrated. I sent them a letter dated July 21, 1998, and I realize I may have been a little professionally snarky in this response. In lieu of giving NORAD what they requested and photocopying the entire JANAP

146(E) document, I instead informed them of the FOIA case I received it under, from the Office of the Assistant Secretary of Defense: FOIA Case #96-F-2515. I then typed in the page that pertained specifically to UFOs and to NORAD, so they had what they needed but nothing more. In other words, in a professional manner but maybe one I regret, I told them to get it themselves. In fairness, I was still seventeen years old going back and forth with NORAD, so to begin with, I did not have much money to print off full manuals as I was still in high school with no job, but second, I had a teenage-level frustration that I had not learned to squash yet. Looking back, this was evidence of that.

The final letter in this exchange came from NORAD dated August 6, 1998. They thanked me for my response and information, then stated the following:

> In the past, we received several similar requests for these "CIRVIS" sighting re-ports and conducted a thorough search at the headquarters, regions and sectors, but failed to come up with any samples, past or present. Apparently there are newer electronic reporting procedures now and these former procedures either are no longer used and/or no longer apply. In any case, any report similar to these former "CIRVIS Reports" are considered NORAD sensitive internal working documents and are not releasable to the general public.

There is a lot to this paragraph, but I will begin with the obvious first line. How, within weeks of my exchanges with them, did they go from not even knowing about JANAP 146 to then stating they had received "several similar requests for these 'CIRVIS' sighting reports" in their next letter? It really is JANAP 146 itself that defines what a CIRVIS sighting report is and where they are supposed to be sent to, so what happened there?

They have stated they never came up with samples of CIRVIS reports, but if newer protocols existed, CIRVIS-like records would not be disclosed. Which is it? They either have them or they don't, but they seem to keep contradicting themselves in not only this letter but in the string of letters that came into my mailbox in the months prior.

Although there were other Air Force regulations and reporting protocols throughout Project Blue Book's era, basically they would say the same thing and just overwrite each other as a new one was published. Most, if not all, of the Air Force regulations were rescinded and cancelled when Project Blue Book closed, and therefore, they all disappeared. However, JANAP 146 remained. In fact, it continued to be updated as late as 1977; eventually it is believed to also have been rescinded, but the exact date of that is unknown.

Despite these regulations being "off the books," we have already seen many UFO-related intelligence reports and documents appear in the files of the

DoD 5040.6-M-1

DECISION LOGIC TABLE
INSTRUCTIONS FOR
RECORDING AND HANDLING
VISUAL INFORMATION
MATERIAL

OCTOBER 21, 2002

ASSISTANT SECRETARY OF DEFENSE
FOR
PUBLIC AFFAIRS

Figure 12.2. Cover page for Department of Defense Manual 5040.6-M-1, Decision Logic Table Instructions for Recording and Handling Visual Information Material.

Defense Intelligence Agency (DIA), National Security Agency (NSA), and the Central Intelligence Agency (CIA) that come well after the dates these manuals and protocols were rescinded. Although I could not find any type of regulation or procedural manual for these records I discussed in previous chapters, I did make an interesting discovery that came many years after Project Blue Book. In fact, it came in the next century.

Department of Defense (DOD) manual 5040.6-M-1 was published on October 21, 2002. It began with a summary to what the manual's purpose was:

If VI [visual information] imagery is to meet the Department of Defense's operational and other needs, DoD camera operators must focus their efforts on capturing specific imagery, and avoid expending time and resources recording other imagery. This Manual, with the short title "DLT," or "Decision Logic Table," helps achieve that goal by providing DoD camera operators with specific guidance on what imagery they should try to capture, and what they should do with it afterwards.

What stuck out to me, when I discovered this document, was the table of contents. Chapter 5 ended with a bizarre reference you would not think to see in a manual written by the DOD in 2002, and it read, "C5.21. UFO and Other Aerial Phenomena Imagery."

I was a bit surprised to see this reference on the table of contents. The Air Force is one branch of the DOD, and it was the DOD that tasked that agency to investigate UFOs decades and decades prior. So, if they concluded UFOs were not real and explained, and they denounced interest, why would the DOD be offering instructions on what to do with UFO photographs?

In chapter 5, this DOD manual explained exactly what to do with them:

C5.21. UNIDENTIFIED FLYING OBJECT (UFO) AND OTHER AERIAL
PHENOMENA IMAGERY

DoD 5040.6-M-1, October 2002

C5.21. UNIDENTIFIED FLYING OBJECT (UFO) AND OTHER AERIAL
PHENOMENA IMAGERY

The following table concerns imagery that records UFOs and other aerial phenomena not obviously identifiable as conventional aircraft or missiles. The table also lists the priority assigned to each category of imagery and provides relevant handling instructions.

Table C5.T21. UFO and Other Aerial Phenomena Imagery

Subject Description	Instructions
5-21-1. Aerial flying objects not obviously identifiable as conventional aircraft	NORMAL. Provide copies or dubs as needed to local and major commands. Handle camera-recorded imagery according to Appendix 2.
5-21-2. Aerial phenomena (including moving lights and similar phenomena)	

Figure 12.3.   Department of Defense Manual 5040.6-M-1, Decision Logic Table Instructions for Recording and Handling Visual Information Material, held instructions on what to do with UFO and Other Aerial Phenomena Imagery.

The following table concerns imagery that records UFOs and other aerial phenomena not obviously identifiable as conventional aircraft or missiles. The table also lists the priority assigned to each category of imagery and provides relevant handling instructions.

Subject Description

5-21-1. Aerial flying objects not obviously identifiable as conventional aircraft

5-21-2. Aerial phenomena (including moving lights and similar phenomena)

Instructions

NORMAL. Provide copies or dubs as needed to local and major commands. Handle camera-recorded imagery according to Appendix 2.

This was a single-page section—in other words, short and sweet—but it outlined where and how to report UFO photographs. This then gave me a lead, as this is a prime example of how the FOIA process works to an investigator. The discovery of this manual allowed me to take that one FOIA request for it and turn it into another asking specifically for records and photographs. Sadly, I was never able to turn up a single photograph ever submitted under DOD manual 5040.6-M-1. I will let you decide on how likely it is that not a single photograph would exist.

I followed the progression of this manual, and in April of 2005, another version was created in the form of DoD 5040.6-M-2. In this version, the section I referenced above was removed. However, a strange reference remained in the "Definitions" section in the beginning of the manual. For the definition of "Documentation Imagery," it explained:

Imagery depicting actual events, activities, phenomena, places, or people recorded primarily to create a record of the subject matter.

The key word here is "phenomena." In the first version of the manual published in 2002, the word "phenomena" was only referenced as part of the UFO photographs; however, it remained while that section was removed. Of course, it could have been an oversight, or it was a key to the fact that the interest to the "phenomena" was still there but may now appear in another manual or regulation. I have yet to find if that exists, but either is a plausible scenario.

DoD 5040.6-M-2 was finally rescinded as well and replaced with what is known as DAA-0330-2013-0014. In this one, there are no references to "UFOs" or "phenomena." It should be interesting to note one possibility here.

When the first manual was written in 2002, The Black Vault and my efforts were about seven years old at that point. The Internet, although very popular, was nothing like it was ten or fifteen years later in regard to sheer volume of users and the accessibility of some information. As people like me were making these discoveries, and highlighting with absolute certainty the UFO interest by all branches of the military and government, I feel they may have felt they needed a change.

There is a huge possibility that at this time, those making decisions to put things online did not realize the effect it would have, wherein people would actually ask questions. That sounds simplistic in nature and silly that this type of mistake would be made. However, we are dealing with a government that still, well into the twenty-first century, is using archaic programming code and dated software to keep track of their records. I will not even begin to bore you with the research I did on the U.S. government's development of HealthCare.gov and the ballooning costs of more than a half a *billion* dollars at the time it was programmed. Yes, it was estimated to cost taxpayers more than $500,000,000 to build a website. Although you may not see a connection there, my overall point is technology and advancements like these have not been historically the U.S. government's strong suit.

So as the manuals were rewritten and republished, references that may cause people like me to ask questions were removed, and those references may have found themselves into other classified versions that never get an online digital footprint. I have sought other types of manuals such as these; however, I have not come up with them. I will let you fill in the blank on whether you feel they may exist.

When I was researching all of this, many of the regulations made sense, especially those that pertained to the Air Force and clearly showed that Project Blue Book would be the recipient of UFO reports. However, JANAP 146 confused that process for me as an investigator because this existed for many years after and pertained to multiple agencies and even America's neighbor to the north—Canada. In addition, there was no mention of Project Blue Book, so where did all of these reports go?

It was this latter fact that made me keep digging for more proof that there was a present-day interest in the UFO phenomenon and that there were more documents than the U.S. government and military wanted to admit. So I looked harder. I filed FOIA requests and began sifting through responses I got until I made a discovery that literally changed my entire perception of UFOs and how involved the United States really was.

CANADA
COMES THROUGH

You just read about a stack of various UFO regulations in the previous chapter. They outlined specifically how to report a UFO and where to report them to. The biggest discovery for me, up until this point, was the existence of JANAP 146. Although written about extensively in UFO literature before I came along, it did show me that there was a lot more going on behind the scenes than we were being led to believe, especially after the run-around at NORAD. History was showing me this, so I pressed on to find irrefutable proof of a "present-day UFO interest," specifically by the United States.

I guess you can call it another hunch that I had, but I was astonished when I discovered that the proof I was actually looking for—actually existed. You just needed to know where to look and how to find it.

Back in the year 2000, I had discovered Air Force Instruction 10-206. In fact, I had discovered this by pure accident. I had revisited JANAP 146 and "CIRVIS" reports in 2000 and decided just to do an Internet search. Google was not really as popular as it is now, so I had used Alta Vista for this particular search. I queried "CIRVIS" and explored what was found. There were a few websites that referenced JANAP 146, even my own, but it was the very last result on the page that stuck out. It read "Air Force Instruction 10-206." I thought there was no way it would actually pertain to CIRVIS. I mean, why would an Air Force manual connect with UFO reports, especially in the year 2000? If it was real, it had to be decades old and not important.

The link was broken, and I couldn't obtain it by clicking on the reference in the search results. I thought that was strange, so I dug deeper. I ended up finding a version of the manual online, from the U.S. Air Force, and sure enough, the document was real, and it was dated from the year 2000.

BY ORDER OF THE
SECRETARY OF THE AIR FORCE

AIR FORCE INSTRUCTION 10-206
15 OCTOBER 2008

Operations

OPERATIONAL REPORTING

COMPLIANCE WITH THIS PUBLICATION IS MANDATORY

ACCESSIBILITY: Publications and forms are available on the e-Publishing website at **www.e-Publishing.af.mil** for downloading or ordering.

RELEASABILITY: There are no releasability restrictions on this publication.

Figure 13.1. Air Force Instruction 10-206 proved to be one of the biggest discoveries I ever made.

When I came across the manual, just as I had previously done with the DOD manuals about UFO photographs, I sifted through the table of contents for clues to what was inside. Obviously, it connected to "CIRVIS" reports somehow, so I figured this would tell me why.

To my surprise, chapter 5 was something I was not quite expecting, especially in an Air Force manual. This was not a "joint publication," nor did it apply to any other country. This was specifically to the Air Force, and chapter 5 was entitled "Communications Instructions Reporting Vital Intelligence Sightings (CIRVIS)."

CIRVIS? That was an uncommon acronym in records outside of JANAP 146, and it reminded me that sometimes UFO documents are not always referred to as "UFO documents." CIRVIS seemingly was an acronym used that could potentially be UFO information. But why was it in an Air Force manual?

Naturally, I quickly went to chapter 5. It said:

5.1. Subject and Purpose. This report provides vital information to the security of the United States and Canada which, in the opinion of the observer, requires very urgent defensive action or investigation by the US and/or Canadian Armed Forces. 5.2. Submitted By. Any Air Force personnel.

Although the manual did not pertain to Canada, it was clear it dealt with the safety of them, along with the United States. The events that were chronicled in a CIRVIS report, according to Air Force Instruction 10-206, may even require military action. When I read this, I knew it had the potential of getting good!

5.6.3.1. Hostile or unidentified aircraft, which appears directed against the United States, Canada, or their forces.

5.6.3.2. Missiles.

5.6.3.3. Unidentified flying objects.

5.6.3.4. Hostile or unidentified military surface vessels or submarines.

5.6.3.5. Any other individual surface vessels, submarines, or aircraft of unconventional design engaged in suspicious activity, observed in an unusual location, or on a course, which may threaten the United States, Canada, or their forces.

Figure 13.2. Chapter 5 of Air Force Instruction 10-206 clearly displayed the USAF was actively interested in and collecting UFO reports as late as 2008.

As I read through the chapter, I found the gem I was looking for. It outlined the types of sightings that were to be reported under this Air Force manual:

5.6.3. Report the following specific sightings:

5.6.3.1. Hostile or unidentified aircraft, which appears directed against the United States, Canada, or their forces.

5.6.3.2. Missiles.

5.6.3.3. Unidentified flying objects.

5.6.3.4. Hostile or unidentified military surface vessels or submarines.

5.6.3.5. Any other individual surface vessels, submarines, or aircraft of unconventional design engaged in suspicious activity, observed in an unusual location, or on a course, which may threaten the United States, Canada, or their forces.

5.6.3.6. Any unexplained or unusual activity, which may indicate a possible attack against or through Canada or the United States (includes the presence of any unidentified or suspicious ground parties in remote or sparsely populated areas, including the polar region).

5.6.3.7. Unlisted airfields, facilities, weather stations, or air navigation aids.

Smack in the middle of the list, as you can see, was "unidentified flying objects." This had to be a mistake, right? I mean, UFOs were explainable and not of interest to the Air Force; yet in this Air Force manual, it outlined how to report them. To make matters even more interesting, Air Force Instruction 10-206 was still very much "on the books" and current. We are not talking about manuals that were written decades before I was even born anymore; we are talking about a present-day, irrefutable piece of evidence that the very agency who founded the "company line" had UFOs in their manuals to be reported well into the twenty-first century.

My next order of business was to find out where these CIRVIS reports were located. Of course, not 100 percent of them would be on UFOs, as evidenced by the list of what they could pertain to, but obviously UFOs were on the list for a reason, and it was something that had to make up some percentage of the overall collection of reports. What percentage that would be remained a mystery.

I sifted through the manual to understand not only *what* was to be reported but *where* it was to be reported to. It was quite clear that CIRVIS reports were to be created by all Air Force personnel if they saw something outlined above, and it was all spelled out with great detail:

5.2. Submitted By. Any Air Force personnel.

5.3. Submitted To:

5.3.1. Airborne reports: US, Canadian military, or civilian communications facility.

5.3.2. Post-landing reports: Commander, North American Aerospace Defense Command (NORAD), Cheyenne Mt, Colorado, or HQ Northern NORAD Region, North Bay, Ontario, Canada, whichever is more convenient. If landing outside Canadian or US territories, submit reports through the nearest Canadian military or diplomatic representative or US.

5.4. When Submitted. As soon as possible after the intelligence sighting.

5.5. How Submitted. Reports are normally UNCLASSIFIED but handled as FOUO.

5.5.1. Use the most rapid means of transmission available. For airborne reports, use the same procedures as for air traffic control. When pilots cannot establish contact with a ground station, make maximum effort to relay the report via other aircraft.

5.5.2. To avoid delays while airborne, repeat the word CIRVIS three times before the message to preempt all other communications (except distress and urgency). If this fails to clear the frequencies, use the International Urgency Signal "PAN" spoken three times. For the ground relay of airborne reports or post-landing reports, use FLASH precedence.

Let me summarize the above for you in the easiest way possible. CIRVIS reports were incredibly important, they were to be submitted by any Air Force personnel by the fastest means possible, and they were to be sent to the North American Aerospace Defense Command (NORAD) for review. These three points are important because it shows the necessity for the reports to be made and who it applied to specifically, and it outlined that the reports were to be going to the one military facility that really is responsible for watching, well, space: NORAD.

NORAD? Again? Just two years prior, I went through the ringer trying to show NORAD that JANAP 146 even existed, since they claimed to not know about it. Then once I proved that, they changed their tune and said they never found any CIRVIS reports within their holdings nor did they find UFO-related information. They, of course, also tried to sell me on the "company line" again in the form of an attached "fact sheet" I was getting so sick of receiving.

I filed another request (made under the NORAD instruction and not FOIA) to NORAD for their CIRVIS reports but got the same response. I crafted the request fairly specifically, having asked for all CIRVIS reports as mandated by Air Force Instruction 10-206. It was clear that NORAD would be the receiving agency, so therefore, *now* you would expect me to get a stack of records as a response because I had the irrefutable proof it should exist. Yet again, that was not the case, and they claimed to have "no records" relating to anything on CIRVIS.

This was one of my biggest discoveries to date, which proved beyond any shadow of a doubt that the U.S. Air Force still held an interest in the topic. This Air Force Instruction had never been known to anyone researching UFOs before. I knew I was on to something big, but I could not get my hands on anything related to CIRVIS. What were the odds that the U.S. Air Force had this manual (previous versions referred to it as "Air Force *Manual* 10-206"), which spelled out CIRVIS and UFOs, and did not collect one single report? The odds of that were astronomical, in my opinion. So what should I do?

The answer came in that original letter I received in 2008 from NORAD, but it took me years to realize it. Let me revisit it and remind you of what it said:

> For your information, Title 5 United States Code (U.S.C.), Section 552, the Freedom of Information Act (FOIA), is a United States (US) statute and is only applicable to US agencies as defined in Title 5 U.S.C., sections 551 and 552. NORAD is a binational command, established by Volume 33, United States Treaties (UST), page 1277, subject to control of both Canadian and US Government agencies as defined in the Act and is subsequently not subject to the US FOIA.

The reason they were not subject to the *United States* FOIA is because they were also under *Canadian* control. So, therefore, U.S. law did not apply. But then I thought to myself, "Does Canada have an equivalent law to the FOIA?"

I did some research, and they sure did. It is called the Access to Information Act or AIA. Although I knew that anyone in the world, no matter where they were located, could utilize the FOIA in the United States, I had no idea if the same applied to the AIA in Canada.

So, being impatient, I did some research and found that the Department of National Defence (DND) would be the likely candidate for having CIRVIS information, as outlined within the JANAP 146 document, so I picked up the phone. I recall being fairly nervous when I made the phone call, as I did not know what to expect. The DND was the equivalent to America's DOD so I was not sure if they would even want to take my phone call or continue to talk to me once they figured out why I was calling.

The phone rang, and a gentleman picked up. Of course, I said hello, but then jumped to my question: "I was wondering, can anyone outside of Canada request information under the Access to Information Act?" I remember the gentleman hemming and hawing, thinking for a moment, and he said verbatim, "Ummm, if the information has been released before, I don't see why not."

Great! That was at least the first step. Being that impatient kid in a candy store, I then asked another question: "Sir, I am actually looking for something called CIRVIS reports—that stands for Communications Instructions . . ." and before I ever finished my sentence, he interrupted me midway through, and he jumped in saying, "Oh yeah! I have those right here!"

Wait—what? He really did say that, and I knew what he said, but I still pretended I did not hear him, so I said, "I'm sorry?" He said, "Yeah, I have them right here. I like to keep these things handy!"

He said it with a tinge of excitement in his voice. I am not sure if that excitement was because he could answer my question right away or if he had a personal fascination with these CIRVIS reports, but regardless, I heard him rustle the papers in his hand.

I needed to act professional, but inside, I wanted to shout. These documents, according to NORAD, did not exist. And yet I called Canada, and they had them on their desks! I took a deep breath and calmly asked how I could get a copy of the CIRVIS records in his hands. He said, "Sure, do you have a Visa?"

Was I sure glad I had a bank account with a bank card at this moment. However, I was fairly nervous about how much they were going to charge me. I asked how many pages he had, and he stated there were "about one hundred." Then I wondered how much he was going to charge me, so I asked.

I am going to tell you now, that during the course of my entire life, at least up until writing this book, this remains the best $3.92 Canadian dollars and cents that I had ever spent. Just as I was about to get off the phone once I gave him my Visa number, he said, "Oh, by the way—this is not all of them!"

"Really?" I questioned back. He said, "Oh yeah, we got boxes of these down at archives." What a loaded thing to end the conversation with! I was excited enough to get these one hundred pages of documents, but to learn there were boxes more . . . that was quite intriguing.

The $3.92 Canadian was charged to my Visa card, and sure enough, weeks later, I received the packet of material. To my surprise, the top of the stack began with Canadian regulations outlining CIRVIS reports, how to make them, and where to send them to. They were worded nearly identically to the U.S. versions I had already found and reinforced the fact that CIRVIS dealt with UFO sightings and were of great importance. The first page held the label of "All documents pertaining to National Defence Policies Concerning Sightings of Unidentified Flying Objects," which indicated what the following pages would contain. The next page gave me the excerpt from the first manual labeled AOC CL 9:

CIRVIS reports should be made immediately upon a vital intelligence sighting of any airborne, waterborne and ground objects or activities which appear to be hostile, suspicious, unidentified or engaged in possible illegal smuggling activity. Examples of events requiring CIRVIS reports are:

- unidentified flying objects;
- submarines or warships which are not Canadian or American;
- violent explosions; and
- unexplained or unusual activity in polar regions, abandoned airstrips or other remote, sparsely populated areas.

When a VERBAL CIRVIS report is received, compile the information in an orderly format and prepare a PRIORITY message as follows;
ACTION: TRANSPORT CANADA // AARBI OTTAWA//
INTERNAL ADDRESS: AOC FILE
SUBJ: CIRVIS CIRVIS CIRVIS
Text should include the following information:
a. identification of reporting personnel / aircraft / etc;
b. brief description of sighting: number, size, shape, etc;
c. position of sighted object or activity;
d. date and time of sighting in UTC;
e. altitude of object;
f. direction of movement of object;
g. speed of object; and
h. any identification.

In addition to this manual, there was another titled "Flight Planning and Procedures Canada and North Atlantic" and labeled "DND Flight Information Publication—GPH 204." It stated:

850. PILOT REPORTS—GENERAL
Pilots are requested to make the following reports in the interest of national security, forest fire and pollution control.

The next section was the following:

851. CIRVIS REPORTS—VITAL INTELLIGENCE SIGHTINGS

The text that followed was verbatim from the first manual I referenced above, so I won't repeat it for you. This made it clear that for national security purposes, the UFO-related CIRVIS reports were to be filed immediately after the sightings took place, and the verbiage existed in multiple manuals to ensure the reports were generated properly and promptly.

What followed next in this packet of material was a stack of UFO-related CIRVIS reports. Therein lay the gold nugget that I was looking for, and this was for a few reasons. First, the documents should not exist, according to NORAD. Recall the letters wherein they stated they had searched for CIRVIS-related reports in the past but found no examples. However, the majority of these documents all said "CIRVIS" at the top, which in itself was defined by all these manuals that I have referenced including JANAP 146, Air Force Instruction 10-206, and others. In these records, it was outlined that NORAD would be the receiving end for all CIRVIS records, and yet NORAD denied they had any of them.

When asked for CIRVIS reports, the Canadian government just simply handed them over. What an amazing revelation—and quite a surprising one. And when sifting through the CIRVIS reports themselves, I was not expecting the wide array of sighting descriptions, just in the few pages I did receive. There were flashing lights in the sky, red objects, football-shaped objects, lights with no discernable shapes, and even a crop circle report.

A crop circle report? This veered well away from the definitions within the manuals that defined CIRVIS, but nevertheless, there it was. What stuck out more than anything, however, was a code at the top of nearly every page.

Similar to other intelligence reports that I referenced in previous chapters, at the top of the CIRVIS reports was a "distribution list." This would indicate where that particular report was sent to for intelligence-gathering purposes.

This included Transport Canada, the Air Operations Center in Ottawa, and an acronym that said "CANR." This stands for the Canadian NORAD Region. Yes, NORAD. That same agency that told me they've looked numerous times in the past and found no CIRVIS reports; here was a stack of them with this NORAD code at the top.

You cannot make this up. This was such proof of a lie that I thought there was some catch or something I was missing, but there is no viable explanation that I could think of that explains this. It was like the American side of NORAD wanted to cover it all up, but going through the Canadian side, they were freely giving it out to those that wanted to pay $3.92 Canadian dollars and cents.

This, for me, was the moment I was waiting for. It proved beyond a doubt that UFO reports were still being collected, and all evidence from the United States showed it was going to one agency that was not subject to the FOIA. Although NORAD attempted to process requests in the "spirit of the FOIA" under NORAD Instruction 35-17, it appeared that attempt was failing.

As the years progressed, I spoke about this entire connection quite frequently at public lectures and even during a few television interviews. It was a fantastic story that really is a bit too good to be true when it comes to proving a present-day cover-up, but all the evidence was there and verifiable.

And one day, when a popular mainstream media newspaper wanted to profile The Black Vault, they asked for the "Top 5 UFO-related documents" I had ever received. My response gave them the CIRVIS connection, and when they went to verify it with the Pentagon, the most astonishing vanishing act began.

THE GREATEST TRICK
OF A MAGICIAN

In Chapter 7, I briefly mentioned my study of magic and what I called the "greatest trick of a magician." To me, that is the ability to make your audience look in your right hand, so they do not see what is going on in your left. I knew the U.S. government employed such tactics in regard to government secrets, but I never imagined the attempt at a complete vanishing act would be added to their repertoire.

I received a phone call in October of 2011 from my friend Lee Spiegel, a journalist for the *Huffington Post* (at the time). He and I had met many times in the past and struck up a friendship due to our desire for factual and verifiable information, rather than wild claims and conjecture.

He asked me if I would be interested in him doing a story for the *Huffington Post* that would highlight The Black Vault and some of the documents I had received. I remember the interview I did with him over the phone, and one of the questions he asked was about the "Top 5 UFO-related documents" I had ever received.

It was a common question for me to be asked, and I loved answering it. This was always an opportunity for me to give out some of my favorites—like the "1976 Iran Incident" document, the Top Secret NSA affidavit, and Air Force Instruction 10-206.

It was the latter that Mr. Spiegel was intrigued by the most. For anyone thinking logically, why would the same agency that denies any interest in the phenomenon have it spelled out in black and white to report it, and to do so urgently and immediately? It did not make sense, so Mr. Spiegel focused in on that document for the course of the rest of the interview.

What I feel like he was impressed by the most, besides the existence of the document, was that I told him he did not have to take my word for it and could download the document itself from the Air Force. I walked him through navigating a very difficult-to-use but public Air Force database.

I walked him directly to Air Force Instruction 10-206. Although I had discovered the manual in 2000, it had been revised multiple times, and on this occasion when Mr. Spiegel downloaded it, it was the 2008 version, which at the time, was the most recent. From 2000 to 2008, during the revisions that this document underwent, I was pleased to say to Mr. Spiegel that the CIRVIS section, chapter 5, and the UFO references were never once taken out.

I bring up these revisions because it is a key point to Air Force Instruction 10-206. The military would actually have a pass if this was simply an overlooked regulation that was never updated, was old, and simply stayed "on the books" as an oversight. However, these revisions proved this was not the case and that CIRVIS, along with the UFO reports, were still of interest to the agency.

Mr. Spiegel was impressed by the fact that, if you knew where to look, you could actually find and download this document with ease directly from the U.S. Air Force. There is the expression "hiding in plain sight," which I feel definitely applies here.

After we got off the phone, he called the Pentagon for comment, like any good investigative journalist would do. He was forced to leave a message, since no one was available to take his call, and he waited for a response. In the meantime, he began writing his article.

He left a couple of messages through the next couple of days, but I was unaware of his attempts to contact the Pentagon during the course of his research and the initial writing stages of his article. Then I received a phone call late at night. I was on the West Coast, and he was on the East Coast, so if it was late for me, it was really late for him. I wondered what he might need, so I answered the phone while I was visiting my sister and her family.

I remember the tone of his voice quite clearly. It was excited and with a tinge of concern. He said, "John, you're not going to believe this!" Of course I was intrigued and said, "What?"

His next words, in my opinion, changed UFOlogy and began a new chapter of the UFO cover-up. He said, "Air Force Instruction 10-206, chapter 5, it's gone!" Gone? There was no way that could be true, as we had just downloaded it within the past week, from the Air Force even, and it was there, specifying UFOs and outlining CIRVIS.

Since I was with family, I told him to let me get home, sit at a computer, and see what I could find. With respect to Mr. Spiegel, I did not quite believe that chapter 5 "was gone," but rather, I assumed Mr. Spiegel followed the wrong link or clicked on the wrong thing and wound up with a different document and did not realize it.

Chapter 5—HURRICANE CONDITION/TROPICAL CYCLONE CONDITIONS OF
READINESS (HURCON/TCCOR) REPORTING   29

    5.1.   OPREP-3B Hurricane/Tropical Cyclone (Typhoon) Conditions of Readiness
        (HURCON/TCCOR).   29

    5.2.   Conditions of readiness are outlined in AFMAN 10-2504; refer to this instruction
        for specific HURCON/TCCOR responses for units.   29

    5.3.   OPREP-3B initial report will be submitted when a commander directs a change
        in readiness condition (T-1).   29

    5.4.   General Reporting: 29

Figure 5.1.   OPREP-3B HURCON/TCCOR Template   30

Figure 5.2.   OPREP-3B HURCON/TCCOR Example   31

Figure 14.1. Proof that after the Air Force received the phone call from the press, profiling my discovery, they changed chapter 5 entirely and deleted all UFO references

When I got home and went back online to see what was going on, I realized Mr. Spiegel was absolutely right. Chapter 5 was completely deleted, and it had been changed to a chapter titled, "Hurricane Condition/Tropical Cyclone Conditions of Readiness (HURCON/TCCOR) Reporting." Hurricanes? Cyclones? How did CIRVIS get changed to that? Immediately, I searched the entire .pdf document for the word "CIRVIS." Gone. I searched for "unidentified." Gone. The entire reference to CIRVIS and UFOs was completely deleted from the record, like it had never existed.

Then Mr. Spiegel got a reply from the Air Force in the form of an e-mail. Air Force Major Chad Steffey told Mr. Spiegel and the *Huffington Post* that the deletion of chapter 5 was merely a coincidence. He also said, "All Air Force Instructions are reviewed/revised on a regular basis (about every two to three years). For this revision, we merely deleted a procedure that did not apply to this AFI. For any other questions about requirements for UFO reporting, I'll have to refer you to NORAD."

NORAD again, huh? Yeah, we all know what will happen if we decide to ask NORAD for an answer, and if you forget, just re-read chapter 11! NORAD claimed no interest in UFOs and claimed they did not have a single CIRVIS record, even in one letter denying they even knew what JANAP 146 was and asking me for a copy.

I believe whole-heartedly this is one of the most intriguing stories I have ever been a part of in more than two decades of research. It proves beyond a doubt that not only is there a present-day interest in the UFO phenomenon, but when pressed, the U.S. military will do anything to cover it all up.

What do you think the odds are of this being all a coincidence? Air Force Instruction 10-206 was discovered by me in 2000. It was updated multiple times, through 2008, and yet CIRVIS and UFOs were never deleted. I inform the *Huffington Post* about it, they begin to ask questions, and within days—not months or a year but days—the entire chapter is deleted and changed to one about hurricanes and cyclones? To me, those odds are so astronomical, it's even more evidence to a blatant cover-up.

After this ordeal, I crafted another FOIA request aimed specifically toward finding records relating to the change. In Air Force FOIA Case 2013-05279-F, I was able to come up with the "change log" to the document. This did not give great detail about the change but did say why it was being omitted:

> Remove non-1C3 AFSC reporting items not required by CJCS or CSAF. Reports including REPOL, MEDREP, CIRVIS are reports owned by Logistics, Medical, and NORTHCOM respectively and do not involve 1C3 action or CJCS or CSAF notification. CIRVIS in particular is no longer required.
> The valid reporting processes need to be absored [sic] by their functional areas (Logistcs [sic] and Medical). CIRVIS no longer exists.

This may be another small stretch, but I have to point it out. You will notice with the above quotes, I left the spelling errors that are in the original document. Although humans make mistakes, and yet again I try not to be a "Grammar Nazi," what do multiple spelling errors in a U.S. military document tell you? Spelling errors do happen but are fairly rare in official documents, and here we have multiple ones in a single sentence. In my personal opinion, this is very indicative of the "rush" nature to get Air Force Instruction 10-206 changed.

If this was a planned omission, I believe that the record would have been changed sometime between 2000 and 2008. However, it was not. It was then changed in 2011, just days after the *Huffington Post* asked about it, but that was all a coincidence, according to the Air Force. Yet, here in the change log, it appears to be incredibly rushed documenting the change.

I try not to read into too much, when looking at evidence to U.S. government cover-ups, but in this particular case, you cannot overlook the evidence. Coincidences happen, but to this degree with such astronomical odds? I just don't buy it.

With the cover-up well under way, and at this point, easily provable, what is the UFO phenomenon? The U.S. government and military alike have tried but failed to prove it does not exist, so what are we dealing with?

DEBUNKING
THE DEBUNKERS

With the evidence at hand, the question truly becomes: what are these UFOs? Since the 1940s, the U.S. government and military have had a strong but convoluted connection to the phenomenon, with no viable answer. Arguably, that connection and ultimately the cover-up began with the Roswell incident, but it has lasted throughout the present day, and it shows no sign of ending anytime soon.

The problem with this particular field of study is that there are no real answers yet. Many have tried to claim they have them, but in the end, we are still left with questions. That should not discourage you from opening another book or reading through UFO witness testimony on the Internet or even conducting your own investigation to see what you might add to the field.

Although we do not have a viable conclusion, we have made leaps and strides getting to where we are today. However, each and every step has been met with those who just will discount anything related to UFOs, a government cover-up, or anyone who has witnessed something strange. We call those people "debunkers." Others may call them "skeptics," but I choose to side on the belief that being a skeptic is actually a good thing. I feel I am myself a skeptic, since it takes a lot for me to believe in something or to consider it strong evidence. "Debunkers" are different, wherein no matter what lies in front of them, they will always have something to say to discredit it, and they will always attempt to disprove it, regardless of evidence. The great thing about all of the evidence that you just read through is you cannot debunk it. It is official, it is real, and anyone reading this can verify it really is there by filing their own request for it.

First, let me stress that what you have just read is simply the tip of the iceberg. There are thousands upon thousands of declassified pages to read, and I have only put forth a small percentage in order not to bring you a 98,000-page editorial. To fit everything into one book is impossible, so I hope the previous chapters motivate you to log on and read some more material.

Second, "debunkers" have tried to say that there is nothing to the phenomenon, that there is no cover-up, and the UFO phenomenon is nothing but a giant hoax or a misidentification of a known, Earth-based aircraft or maybe a space object like a meteor or a planet. It does not matter what shred of evidence, testimony, or declassified document you put in front of them. They will always tell you why it cannot be true. I am not exaggerating when I say that it feels like with some debunkers, if an alien came down and slapped them across the face, they will explain by what alternative means they got the pain in their cheek and will explain away the illusion of a slapping alien as nothing more than a short-term psychosis that quickly passed.

I'll dissect a bit of the "debunking" argument, and first I will deal with their claim that is there is no cover-up. What you just read gives ample evidence that *something* is being covered up. We do not know exactly what, but something is clearly being hidden. That is evidenced by thousands upon thousands of pages of documents that remain fully or partially classified and withheld from the public. That is all the evidence you need that there is an active cover-up; but a cover-up of what?

"Debunkers" often will refer to some of their "go-to" explanations for what the UFO phenomenon is. Most commonly, they dismiss many UFO sightings reported as misidentified military aircraft or secret technology that the public may not be privy to. Although I do not argue that many sightings from "people on the street" may be such a misidentified aerial vehicle in the sky, what happens when the military itself is seeing the objects and they cannot explain them on any level of military intelligence?

Of course, "Bob" sitting on his porch in the middle of a rural area could absolutely witness the testing of a fast, low-flying aircraft, and he just does not know how to identify it, so therefore it has to be "alien." That is, sadly, a larger percentage of UFO sightings reported by everyday people than you might want to think. Maybe not always a "Top Secret" aircraft, but more times than not, a witness sees something they do not see every day and mistakes it for something out of this world. These cases can mostly be adequately explained given the appropriate amount of evidence. Yet, when you have highly trained military pilots and personnel that witness the phenomenon, what then is the explanation for that?

I believe one point that has to be made is that all military pilots are not privy to everything that may fly in the sky. That is not to discredit their sighting, but an F-16 pilot may not fully be aware of the Top Secret military aircraft being tested around his particular flight path. However, when you dissect the blacked-out documents and the recounted tales within the ones that are not so redacted, you paint an amazing story, and that is that the military itself has very little idea what these UFOs are. They cannot identify them, and these cases remain within their files as "unidentified" and they lack any viable explanation.

I believe that if a military pilot did witness a Top Secret piece of technology being tested in the air, there would not be the tone that many of these records are written in. There would be more definitive proof that, as the years and decades passed, we have more evidence that a pilot's UFO encounter was nothing more than the "Top Secret Project X Plane" or whatever name it may have. Yet no one can cite a single example of that, and most of these encounters remain unexplained and in many cases still classified, with no indication that the UFO was "our own."

The only attempt at that was the CIA tweeting out UFOs through the 1950s and the "fact" that they were nothing more than secret flights of the U-2. However, I showed very convincing proof that there was actually no way that could be true. So, therefore, we are left with the question still unanswered.

I will cut to the chase at this point. The burning answer that we all want is that it *is* aliens. For more than twenty years, I have wrestled with that and have tried to figure out if that really could be the answer. And to help me inch toward figuring it all out—I had a lot of luck on my side.

In addition to the U.S. government document research, I began appearing on various television shows throughout networks like the History Channel, Discovery Channel, and many others. Along the way, I met some amazing television producers, one of which came into the restaurant I was bartending at for some margaritas and offered me a job. I will leave it up to you to decide whether or not it was the tequila talking, or if he genuinely wanted me to join his team, but I was twenty-one years old at the time, I did not want to bartend forever, and I absolutely loved the idea of making television.

The lights, the cameras, the people, and the end product—I fell in love with it all. So when I poured his last margarita, he asked me to come in the next day for that interview. I was more than happy to do it!

I got the job and worked my way up from there. Within a couple years, I became what is known as a "supervising producer" and also wrote and directed various documentaries and shows for different networks. Now, I am telling you about this part of my life because working on these shows allowed me to literally research "full time" various aspects to answering that "alien" question.

Being a producer and writer is an amazing gig to have. You get to dive deep into whatever the topic at hand is, and you put together a package that is interesting, exciting, captivating, and whatever other word you can think of to help keep you glued to the screen. I began my television career with UFO documentaries but branched out to other areas as well, including a series on military generals, a documentary on secret societies like the Freemasons, and even multiple scientific-based shows based on the universe.

This leads me to why I am telling you this. Working on these types of documentaries allowed me, from a personal standpoint, to bridge the gap between the UFO documents I was uncovering and some of the most cutting-edge scientific discoveries that astronomers and astrobiologists were making.

Of course, I had a job and that was to make a great show, but in my mind, I was trying to piece together the skeptical arguments *against* an "alien" connection to UFOs; but I could not make that connection. The skeptical argument and debate became less likely, and it was not possible to just dismiss an "alien" connection.

As I explained already, I have had quite a few UFO-related documentaries credited to my name on networks you probably have seen. However, in addition to that, I also got to write and direct multiple shows that dealt with astrobiology, alien life, and the science of the cosmos.

When I say "alien life," I am not referring to the abduction phenomenon or extraterrestrials visiting planet Earth. What I mean is I got to dive deep into the astrobiology of how an alien life form would flourish in the first place. One series, I felt I had to get my PhD in astrobiology and astrophysics in about ten days. That sounds like an exaggerated joke, but I do feel I was a few units away when I created that show!

It was an insane project, in which I created a hypothetical chunk of the universe, with five different fictional planets, and each had an alien life form. Based on the varying characteristics of gravity, distance from its star, planet density, and so on, each life form was very different.

This show allowed me to fully understand the science and math behind alien life but also the reality of what is possibly out there—and what is not. When I juxtaposed that with the U.S. government and military documents I received, I had to bridge some gaps with common sense and logic, but when I did, it all made sense.

Debunkers are not looking at the bigger picture. You tell them the sky is blue— they will argue it is red, just because they can. Show them a photo of a dog—they will tell you it is a cat because of various lighting angles and digital glitches and the likeliness that it is a hoax. Of course, that is a bit of an exaggeration, but my over-all point is they will argue just about anything that is put in front of them. They never take into account that they can see the sky is blue and they can compare the dog photo to that of an actual dog. Away from being facetious, they also ignore amazing scientific discoveries and advancements that people much smarter than I have made in regard to science and alien life. During the course of producing these television shows, I was able to sit down with Dr. Michio Kaku, Dr. Geoffrey Marcy, Dr. Seth Shostak, Neil deGrasse Tyson, and so many others who showed me that the science is there for UFOs to be real (but they never really actually say "UFOs"). Even though some of these brilliant minds do not want anything to do with the phenomenon, and they even try to discredit it, it is their words that make me believe more there is an alien connection to this entire phenomenon. They may hate me for saying they play a role in my personal hypothesis, but it is very true. You just need to think outside the box.

Let me be clear here, and say I am not 100% convinced the UFO phenom-enon is "aliens" visiting Earth. I want to be blunt, because there should be no twist of words. What I am saying, is when you deal with the evidence and all possible conventional explanations, the "alien" one is the only one that makes sense. What "debunkers" do not want to realize is provable science does not lie—and neither does history. The documents have shown me that the UFO phenomenon is very real. What science then shows me is that the extraterrestrial connection is the most plausible out of all other possible scenarios.

When you look at the evidence presented in the previous chapters, you will conclude various things depending on your mindset. Some will be convinced that the UFO phenomenon *is* connected to an alien presence, while others will still question what UFOs truly are. I like when people question because it makes me work harder at proving what I feel I have already realized. Questioning forces me to collect more and more evidence to prove it all, not only to myself but to everyone who visits The Black Vault or opens up this book or books like it. So I will direct the rest of the book to those who still have questions.

I deal with everything as a small-step process. I know this is not technically the "scientific method," but it is one I feel works well for me. You need to inch yourself toward a conclusion; don't jump. Jumping is where you miss quite a bit, and "debunkers" will have a field day slapping down your theories or con-clusions. Inching there, and proving every inch along the way, allows you to become untouchable by those "debunkers."

Let us inch toward a viable conclusion. Wherever you are on the spectrum of belief, I hope you can walk away from this book realizing there is a cover-up and the UFO phenomenon is real, whatever it may be. That is your first inch and one that is easily provable by documented evidence.

Now, back to that pressing question, which is: can it be aliens? With your first inch proven, and proof that a UFO cover-up exists, what exactly is being hidden? "Debunkers" claim the phenomenon is Top Secret technology or misidentified aircraft. Well, we've already debunked that one, but let's do it again for fun. When the military sees an unknown, and it is verified by radar, you have a physical craft of some kind. When it performs maneuvers or reaches speed beyond the known capability of human technology, then you have a physical unknown that is beyond explanation by conventional means. Craft seen by human eyeballs and radar, going at speeds greater than what the *Guinness Book of World Records* had ever registered by a matter of decades, proves the phenomenon is real and beyond our capability. In the military's own files, if they do not identify it, chances are it is not theirs. It is safe to move on from that theory.

These facts give you another inch. You can safely rule out "Top Secret" technology that may be misidentified by "Farmer Bob," and you can rule out hallucinations, meteors, or any other Earth-based piece of technology or space-based object. No meteor makes a right-angle turn, stops in midair, or increases or decreases speed at the same time it shuts down another encroaching jet aircraft. It just is not done, nor does any of it make sense. Therefore, this inch is now provable, verifiable, and irrefutable just by using science and logic.

Of course, there is a chance that another country is flying their technology over these areas, whether it be inside the United States or beyond, but that is also unlikely. When the military encounters jets, aircraft, or even drones, military pilots can often identify those at first glance. They are trained to look for such technology, and therefore it is highly unlikely that another country has produced something so far advanced, with such capability, that a U.S. military pilot is flabbergasted to the point of not being able to determine what it is. Discounting a foreign military piece of technology offers another inch closer to the truth.

Moving on, what are we left with? Even if we discount a large percentage of these documented encounters within classified (records we have not even seen yet) and formerly classified documents (that have been released) as being something mundane, we are still left with a large enough number of cases to question what the phenomenon truly is, and why the U.S. government and military are actively covering it up.

Back to those brilliant minds I talked about earlier. Speaking with many of these scientists for various shows taught me a few things that play a crucial role into defining what the UFO phenomenon really is, and they never even mentioned the words "unidentified flying objects" or "UFOs." They have proven, within their own careers, that science has been wrong many times in the past. Science has had research, theories, and even scientific fact and principles over-turned as more advancement is made in various fields of study. This history being rewritten all the time should show us that science does not have all the answers. In fact, one thing I took away from speaking with these scientists dur-ing the course of these television programs is that we have more questions about the cosmos than we do answers.

In the same breath, they (the experts) are largely discounting the UFO phe-nomenon being connected to aliens. However, you just cannot do that, if you can't even understand how to set a human foot on the closest planetary neighbor like Mars.

The biggest argument from the experts has always been that the technology required to traverse even just our own solar system would take too long to make it sensible and therefore it is not possible. Let us all keep in mind, man could not even fly before 1903, which is just a little more than a century ago. Since that day that the Wright brothers took flight, we have created jets that fly faster than sound and created rockets that carried man to the moon. We have landed scientific rovers on Mars, and a manmade object known as Voyager 1 has trav-eled more than 13.4 billion miles from Planet Earth, as of October of 2018.

That's all within 1.15 centuries on Earth, or just more than eleven and a half decades. Sure, that may sound like a long time to you, but on the scale of the universe we live in, that is nothing. In fact, the universe itself is believed by some estimates to be 13.8 billion years old. Imagine how much time that really is. In fact, that number that the universe has been around is 120,000,000 times what it has taken humanity to achieve the above-referenced milestones. Really think about that because that plays a crucial role in what I am about to say next.

There have been scientific equations, like the Drake equation, that calculate the number of planets there are in the visible universe. Of course, there are argu-ments on what formula is most accurate and what variable used to calculate the number of planets is more or less likely to contribute to the answer, but Robert Frost, instructor and flight controller at NASA, answered the very question on the number of planets calculated in our universe. Published in *Forbes Magazine* on November 15, 2017, Mr. Frost was quoted as saying the following:

What they do know is that based on measurements of portions of the sky and extrapolation, that there are about 100 billion stars in our galaxy and up to 10 trillion galaxies in the universe. That means up to 1,000,000,000,000,000,000, 000,000 stars. About 7.6% percent of those stars are class G stars (like our Sun).

We haven't been to any of those stars to see if they have solar systems like ours. But we have been studying a very small portion of the sky in the constellation Cygnus, using the Kepler telescope. Kepler doesn't allow us to visually see planets around far away stars, but it allows us to detect changes in the light coming from those stars caused by planets passing in front of the star. From this analysis, the estimates are now that almost all class G stars have at least one planet.

That means there are up to 76,000,000,000,000,000,000,000 stars similar to ours and almost all of them have some form of planets. Based on the Kepler observations, it is now estimated that a quarter of those stars have at least one rocky planet similar in size to the Earth and in the habitable zone.

That means there are up to 19,000,000,000,000,000,000,000 stars similar to ours with at least one planet similar to Earth.

As I mentioned, scientific debates ensue on the exact calculations, but even given a 10 percent, 25 percent, heck, even a 50 percent room for margin of error, you are talking about a considerable number of stars and planets.

To finalize this point on how large, vast, and unknown our universe is, one of my favorite stories is about the Hubble Deep Space Field. The scientific experiment was pretty straightforward. Scientists used the Hubble Space Telescope and, over the period of ten days, took 342 long-exposure photographs of a dark pinpoint in the night sky. The area was so small, it is estimated to be about a 24 millionth portion of the night sky. In this area, the size of a pinpoint to the human eye, there were very few faint-looking stars that were visible. Scientists did not know what to expect but zeroed in on this dark field on the cosmos and began taking photographs.

In the end, the 342 were compiled, and they display an extraordinary array of galaxies. In fact, the photographs revealed more than three thousand galaxies—not planets or stars but galaxies—in this pinpoint of the night sky. Each galaxy is believed to have approximately one hundred billion stars like our own galaxy, if not more. Let me stress that—approximately one hundred billion stars in each of the three thousand galaxies . . . all in the pinpoint of the night sky.

How is any of that possible, let alone fathomable? OK, you get it and I get it: the universe is vast. So what? We all knew that, right? Yes, we kind of did, but the math is just too amazing not to write out in text form. So, that aside, how does it pertain to UFO documents?

The answer to that is easy: intelligence. Scientists believe that life in the universe, let alone intelligent life, has yet to be discovered. However, from a purely mathematical standpoint, what are the astronomical (sorry, pun intended) odds that we really are alone? If you still are not sure, go back and re-read the last couple of pages, and tell me you honestly think that mathematically we can be.

That inch, the one that gives mathematical credence to intelligence life in the universe, is easily proven. So we move forward. The next inch is the scientific probability that can prove alien life *really is* out there in the vastness of space. This goes hand in hand with the math part but is slightly different, as it deals with the pure understanding of life itself.

Scientifically, life is complex yet simple. Rather than write a scientific textbook, I will say that in order to get life, you need the perfect conditions. In order to have the perfect condition, you need a planet to sit in the "Goldilocks Zone" or "Habitable Zone" of a star. This means, that around every star, and yes, I mean *every* star, there is a perfect sweet spot a certain distance from that star for a planet to be in to sustain life. In our own solar system, Earth obviously sits in that zone. Venus, our neighbor toward the sun, is just outside it, sitting too close to the sun, making it too hot. Mars, sitting just outside it, away from the sun, is a bit too cold to sustain life.

This perfect habitable zone is defined by the sun's magnitude, heat, and ultimate lifespan. A sun that dies too early does not allow life to form. Of course, there are other variables, but for our purpose here, that defines where a planet needs to sit.

Now, let's go back to those numbers of stars in the solar system, and the fact that space-based telescopes like the Hubble and more recently the Kepler telescope have made amazing discoveries of Earth-like planets around neighboring stars. In fact, scientists are discovering Earth-like planets around nearly every star they study, which makes that math and the scientific probability that a planet sits within the perfect sweet spot for life much more likely.

It does not take a mathematical or scientific genius to digest this. If you're like me, you won't be able to truly fathom these numbers; they are just simply too large. However, when you apply just a little common sense, we know for a fact there is going to be a percentage of planets within the "Goldilocks Zone," and given enough time, there will be life that will flourish. Give it more time, it may evolve into intelligence, and they themselves may have their own space race, they may leave their planet, and they may even leave their own solar system.

We are now an inch closer to understanding this technology. Mathematically and scientifically, we can safely assume life is out there in some form and with some leeway even accept intelligent life is out there. Of course, this is a bit of a leap from what we understand, but common sense and logic pretty much tell you that is not unlikely. Now the question—can they traverse the stars?

This brings me full circle back to the intelligence strides that we have made on Planet Earth. In just more than a century, we have gone from walking on the dirt to flying faster than sound and landing technology on our planetary neighbors.

Where will we be in another one hundred years? One thousand years? One hundred thousand years? As long as we don't destroy ourselves, where will we be in one million years?

Those questions are hard to comprehend, but one million years is kind of the snap of a finger in space time. In a universe 13.8 billion years old, for one civilization to have a one-million-year (or more) head start is beyond plausible and, to be honest, quite likely. Their technology and capability would be far beyond twenty-first-century human engineering and, in many ways, may not even be recognized by the human eye.

Now we will go back to the documents. "Debunkers" often focus on simply one aspect to a UFO case, and if they can doubt it, they will and they will discredit the entire event. With the U.S. government and military files, we can conclude this is a technology that far surpasses human capability. There is not one or two cases proving that, but many that cannot be dismissed. We can conclude that the U.S. military, in the majority of the cases, fails to identify what the phenomenon truly is. They have tried but fell short of documenting explanations for many of these UFO encounters, like the CIA did with the flights of the U-2. The more the U.S. government speaks about the phenomenon, the more they goof up and make it more intriguing.

In the end, you have a phenomenon that has no viable explanation. When you deal with every skeptical explanation for UFOs, every attempt by a "debunker" to dismiss this field, they all fall like dominoes. None of their explanations make sense when you apply logic, common sense, and a basic understanding of science and math. The only one that has merit is a conclusion that there is an extraterrestrial presence. I have tried long and hard to dismiss that as being the front runner, but when you look at *all* the evidence and you consider *all* the possibilities, that does stand out as the one with the most promise behind it.

The UFO phenomenon remains one of the most classified topics within the holdings of the U.S. government. Time and time again you can prove lie after lie. When the heat gets turned up, and the public is about to hear about UFO reporting regulations, the U.S. military simply deletes it all and says that it was only a coincidence.

You cannot argue that a cover-up ensues, not just in the 1940s or the 1950s but through to the present day. Why is that? For a topic that the U.S. military claims is all hallucinations, swamp gas, and the Planet Venus somehow making a right-angle turn, they are involved in one heck of a controversy!

If not connected to extraterrestrials, then what? I am open to any possibility that makes sense, and I have tried for years to get beyond the whole "alien thing." Debunkers debunk, and many times, they are not wrong. However, when you look at the documented evidence and piece together the evidence like a puzzle, you start putting together an amazing picture. What I have discovered time and time again, however, is that the "amazing picture" that forms when you piece it all together is simply the piece to an even bigger puzzle. I have no idea when it may be all put together.

The UFO phenomenon is one of the most fascinating and intriguing topics you could ever dive into. I hope you all can see the blatant attempt outlined in the past fifteen chapters at what is one of the biggest provable cover-ups in the history of the United States. Now, we just need to keep asking questions until we finally get some of the black lifted and inch one step closer to figuring out what it all means.

I wish you all my best on your journey toward the truth . . . and thank you for taking a brief peek into mine.

INDEX

Access to Information Act (AIA), 145–46
Adamski, George, 29
A.E.C. Installation, 82
aerial phenomena imagery, 137–38
aircraft: Bell X-1, 83; F-4 Phantom, 48, 50, 107; helicopters, 64, 66–68; KC-97, 7; McDonnell F-101A "Voodoo," 119; military, 156–57; SR-71 Blackbird, 119; Su-22, 56; U-2 jet, 122–24, 157, 164; X-43, 83–84
Air Force Base penetration, 64, *65*, 66–73, 84–86, 88–89; Cannon AFB, 71–72; Eglin AFB, 72–73; Loring AFB, 64, *65*, 66–69; Malmstrom AFB, 69–70, 88–89; Minot AFB, 85, 87; RAF Woodbridge, 75–77; Warren AFB, 84–85; Wurtsmith AFB, 69
Air Force Global Weather Central (AFGWC), 71–72
Air Force Historical Research Agency (AFHRA), *23*
Air Force Instruction 10-206, 141, 142–43, *142*, *143*, 145, 152; revisions and deletions, 152–54
Air Force *Manual* 10-206, 145

Air Force Office of Special Investigations (AFOSI), 88
Air Force Regulation 200-2, 127–28, 131
alien codes, *106*
aliens: anthropomorphic dummy explanation, 5–7; as intelligent life, 101–2, 162–64; possibility of, 161–62; witness testimonies, 7–8
Alvarez, Luis, 21

Berkner, Lloyd, 21
The Black Vault, 39–40, 104, 138, 148, 151, 159
Blanchard, "Butch," 1
Bolender, Carroll H., 24, 52
Bolender Memo, *25*
Border Patrol, 66
Brazel, William "Mack," 1

Campaigne, H., 105
Canada: Access to Information Act (AIA), 145–46; and NORAD, 64, 67, 132–33, 148: UFO sightings, 55, 78
Canadian NORAD Region (CANR), 148
Cannon Air Force Base, 72

CAUS vs. NSA, 98–99

Center for UFO Studies (CUFOS), 20

Central Intelligence Agency (CIA), 20, 21, 36, 157, 164; collection of UFO intelligence by, 120, 122; declassified 2011 report, 123; FOIA requests to, 113–116, 124, 126; materials given to Gersten, 113–16; materials post 1980, 114–16; memorandum on UFO report, 120, *121*, 122: publication of article by Gerald Haines, 122–23; Report of the Commission to Assess the Ballistic Missile Threat to the United States, 94–95; Robertson Panel, 21–24, 35; Twitter and emails, 123–26: unclassified document from September 1957, 116–19

"The CIA's Role in the Study of UFOs, 1947–89--A Die-Hard Issue," 36

Citizens Against UFO Secrecy (CAUS), 98, 104; suit against NSA, 98–99

Clinton, William Jefferson "Bill," 110

Cold War, 94

Communications Instructions for Reporting Vital Intelligence Sightings (CIRVIS), 131–32, 142–43, 145; CIRVIS reports, 143–44: deleted from Air Force Instruction 10-206, 152–53; reports from Canada, 146–48

communications intelligence (COMINT), 99, 101, 108, *109*, 111

Condon Committee, 31

Cooper Nuclear Station, 90–93, *91*

crash test dummies, 6–7

debunkers, 155–56, 158–59, 160, 164. *See also* Hynek, J. Allen

Defense Intelligence Agency (DIA), 47, 50, *53*, 63, 97; FOIA requests to, 51; sarcastic tone of reports, 56–59, *58*

Department of Defense (DOD): FOIA requests to, 74–75; Manual 5040.6-M-1, *136*, 137–38, *137*; Manual 5040.6-M-2, 138

Department of National Defence (DND; Canada), 145–46

documentaries, 157–58

document classifications: Confidential, 60, 83, 107; declassified, *6*, 13, *22*, 52, *53*, 71, 73, *74*, 75, *75*, 81, 89, 95, 98, 107, 110, 111, 123, 156, 169; Secret, *22*, 60, 61, 63, 88, 101, 104, 107, 116, 117, 119, 123; Top Secret, 60, 61, 82, 83, 97, 99, 101, 104, 105, 107, 108, *109*, 111, 151, 157, 160; Unclassified, 26, 29, 59, 83, 99, 105, 107, 115, 116, 117, 119, 122, 144

Drake equation, 161

Eglin Air Force Base, 72–73

Eldridge, George, 88

e-mails, 125–26, *125*

Executive Order 12958, 110

extra-terrestrial intelligence, 101–2. *See also* aliens

Federal Aviation Administration (FAA), 66

Federal Bureau of Investigation (FBI), 2, 3, 66

flight speed records, 83–84

Flying Saucers are Real (Keyhoe), 39

FOIA. *See* Freedom of Information Act (FOIA)

Ford, Gerald, 67

Foreign Broadcast Information Service (FBIS), 115, 122

Fort Richie, 72–73

Freedom of Information Act (FOIA): author's initial requests, 9, 47; exemptions, 59; requests to Air

Force Historical Research Agency, 23; requests to CIA, 113–16, 124, 126; requests to DIA, 51; requests to DOD, 74–75; requests to NORAD, 133–35; requests to NSA, 108; requests to Nuclear Regulatory Commission, 89–90, 93; requests to OASD, 62, 63; requests to Space Command, 77–78; requests to U.S. Air Force, 11–12, 154; requests to WPAFB, 11–14; requirements and procedures, 13, 57, 98, 108–10; and UFO investigation, 35–36

Friedman, Stanton, 7

Frontiers of Science magazine, 105

Frost, Robert, 161

General Accounting Office (GAO) investigation, 4–5

Gershater, Ben Z. M., 32–34

Gershater reports, 32–34

Gersten, Peter, 105, 113

Goldilocks Zone, 163

Goudsmit, Samuel A., 21

Habitable Zone, 163

Haines, Gerald K., 36, 122–23

Halt, Charles, 75–77

Halt memo, *76*

Haut, Walter, 2

Hess, Seymour, 102

hoaxes, 28, 31, 43, 156

Hubble Deep Space Field, 162

Hynek, J. Allen, 16, 18–19, 21, 24, 39, 102, 129; correspondence with Quintanilla, 30–31: participation in UFO research, 19–20, 31–32

Internet information, 134, 138–39

Iran Incident (1976), 48–51, *49*, *51*, 107, 151

JFK assassination, 15

Johnson, Kelly, 123

Joint Army Navy Air Force Publication (JANAP) 146, 130–31, 134–35, 141, 143–44, 146

Kaku, Michio, 159

Keyhoe, Donald, 38–39 ·

"Key to Extraterrestrial Messages," 105, *106*

Loring Air Force Base, 64, *65*, 66–69

Los Alamos National Laboratory, 81, 82–83

Macdonald, James E., 102

Malmstrom Air Force Base, 69–70, 88–89

Mandatory Declassification Review (MDR), 109–11

Manhattan Project, 81

Marano, Carmon, 28–29, 32, 36

Marcel, Jesse, 1–2

Marcy, Geoffrey, 159

Mckee, William F., 23

Meiwald, Frederick, 88

Mercer, Rob, 27, 32

meteorites and meteors, 29, 32, 55, 84

military aircraft. *See* aircraft

military bases, 36; Fort Richie, 73; Project Blue Book files on, 84–85. *See also* Air Force Base penetration

Minot Air Force Base, 85, 87

National Academy of Sciences, 10

National Archives and Records Administration (NARA), 11–12, 15, 26, 84

National Electronics Conference, 31

National Military Command Center (NMCC), *65*, *68*, 73

National Reconnaissance Office (NRO), 36

national security, 26, 44, 59, 64, 81, 97, 99; official denial of threat, 10, 23, 24

National Security Agency (NSA), 97–98, 105, 109, 111; FOIA requests to, 108; letter pertaining to lost documents, *112*

newspaper articles, 52, 114–16, 122

North American Aerospace Defense Command (NORAD), 132–35, 144, 148, 153; FOIA requests to, *133–35*

northern lights, 70

NSA Technical Journal, 105

Nuclear Regulatory Commission (NRC), 89–90, 93, 94, 97

nuclear storage facilities, 81–82, 84, 89–90

Office of the Assistant Secretary of Defense (OASD), 62, 63, 97, 135, *136*

Operation High Dive, 7

OXCART program, 123

Page, Thornton, 21

Project Blue Book: closure of, 9–11, 24–26, 44, 45, *46*: conclusions, 10–11; fact sheet on UFOs, 11; failure as scientific investigation, 20, 21, 27, 44, 47; files on military base sightings, 84–85; as government's "final word," 14; inaccuracies and inconsistencies in, 15, 123; scope of, 15, 16; summary, 63; UFO investigations, 32–36. *See also* Hynek, J. Allen

Project Grudge, 9, 12, 16, 23

Project Moon Dust, 52–54, *53*

Project Sign, 9, 12, 16, 23

Quintanilla, Hector, 29–32

radar screen photograph, *86*, 87

RAF Woodbridge, 75–77

Ramey, Roger, 1

Raven Rock Mountain Complex, 74–75, *74–75*

Robertson, Howard P., 21

Robertson Panel, 21, 23, 35; cover page (declassified), *22*; report, 24

Rollins, Jesse, 93

Roswell Army Air Field (RAAF), 2

"Roswell incident," 1, 2; destruction of documents, 4–5; FBI teletype, 3; GAO investigation, 4–5: official explanations for, 5, 7; Wright Field investigation, 2, 4

The Roswell Report: Case Closed (U.S. Air Force), 5, 7

The Roswell Report: Fact Versus Fiction in the New Mexico Desert (U.S. Air Force), 5

Salas, Robert, 88–89

Samford, John A., 38, 43

satellites, 29

Shields, Henry S., 107

Shostak, Seth, 159

Site R, 74–75, *74–75*

sonic boom, 55

Space Command, 77–79

Spiegel, Lee, 151–53

Steffey, Chad, 153

Taylor, Nick, 93

technology: alien capabilities, 26, 164; nuclear, 81; from other countries, 52, 160; present-day capabilities, 161; secret, 156, 157, 160: and space travel, 161, 163–64; unexplained, 47, 50, 52; use by U.S. government, 122, 139

temperature inversion analysis, 70–74

Todd, Robert, 24

Twitter, 123–24

Tyson, Neil deGrasse, 159

U-2 jet airplanes, 122–24, 157, 164

The UFO Experience: A Scientific Inquiry (Hynek), 18–19

UFO fact sheet, 9, *10*, 11, 12, 15, 19, 26, 64, 134, 145

"UFO Hypothesis and Survival Questions," 101, *103*

UFO investigations: discontinuation of, 10: official approach to, 16, 19–20; by University of Colorado, 10; by the U.S. Air Force, 9–10. *See also* Project Blue Book

UFO Magazine, 12

UFO phenomenon: attempts to debunk, 16, 24, 156; as classified topic, 122, 164; confirmation of, 20, 24, 54, 70, 159–60; interest in, 2, 23, 134, 153, 154, 165; and the NSA, 98; official approach to, 9, 11, 19, 24, 32, 38–39, 52, 61, 77–78, 89, 101, 104, 134, 154, 161; shedding light on, 164: as threat, 21, 26, 56, 62, 77; ubiquitous nature of, 36, 62–63, 97; US military and government coverup of, 160. *See also* debunkers; UFO sightings

UFO records: distribution list of reports, 50–51, *51*, 60–61, 62, 65–66, 67, 131–32; instructions for handling UFO imagery, 137–38, *137*; lost files, 26, *32*–33, 111, 148; protocols for writing, 127–32, 147; redacted material, 57–61, *58*, *60*: sarcastic tone of, 56–59, *58*; weather conditions in, 72, 74, 129. *See also* document classifications

UFO research organizations, 61. *See also* Center for UFO Studies (CUFOS); Citizens Against UFO Secrecy (CAUS)

UFOs: caused by "temperature inversions," 71–74; fear of Soviet origins, 117, 119; identified as aircraft, 122–24, 157, 164; identified as ball lightning, 87–88; identified as balloons, 2, 5, 29, 108; identified as clouds, *32*; identified as ICBM missiles, 94–95; identified as meteorites/meteors, 29, 32, 55, 84; identified as northern lights, 70; identified as plasma, 87–88; identified as satellites, 29, 32, 57; identified as space debris, 57; official explanations for, 16, 35, 63–64, 70–71, 87, 101–2, 119, 156, 164; Project Blue Book explanations for, 16, 29, 32; speed of, 82, 83–84, *118*, 119, 124

"UFO's and the Intelligence Community Blind Spot to Surprise or Deceptive Data," *103*–4, 104

UFO sightings, 2, 38, 148; 1947–1969, *37*; in Canada, 55, 78; in China, 30–31, 61; by commercial airlines, 82; at Cooper Nuclear Station, 90–93; dogfight with military aircraft, 56; by Florida airmen, 33–34; in Ghana, 57–58; in Hamburg, NY, 40–43; hoaxes, 28, 31, 43, 156; in Iran, 48–51, *49*, *51*, 107, 151; in Jordan, *60*; at Los Alamos, 82–83; at military bases, 36, 73; in New York, 116–17; by NY amateur photographer, 40–43; in Peru, 56; Roswell, 1, 7–8; by Russian radar crews, 94–95; simple explanations for, 156; in Spain, 54–55; summary from Space Command, 78–79; tracking record, *118*, 119; "unclassified," 59; "unidentified," 10–11, 19, 30–31, 52, 57, 59, 61, 128; in United Kingdom, 75–77; "unknown," 16–18; over Washington, D.C., 21, 23, 36, 38; by Zamora, 16–18. *See also* Air Force Base penetration

UFO traces: burned brush, 16–17; impressions in the ground, 16–17, 55, 77; radar screen photographs, *86*, 87; Roswell debris, 1–2

University of Colorado, 10

US Air Defense Command, 116–17

U.S. Air Force: FOIA requests to, 11–12, 154; UFO fact sheet, 10, 26, 64, 134; UFO investigations, 9–10, 16

Warren Air Force Base, 84–85

weather conditions, 72, 73, 129. *See also* temperature inversion analysis

Wilcox, George, 1

Wright Field, 2, 4. *See also* Wright Patterson Air Force Base (WPAFB)

Wright Patterson Air Force Base (WPAFB), 27–28, 83; FOIA requests to, 11–12, 13–14; page denied by, *14*

Wurtsmith Air Force Base, 69

Yeager, Chuck, 83

Yeates, Eugene F., 98–99

Yeates affidavit, 99, *100*, 101, 104, 105, 111

Zamora, Lonnie, 16–18

ABOUT THE AUTHOR

Starting at the age of fifteen, **John Greenewald Jr.** was struck with a curiosity that led off a lifelong journey. First researching the UFO phenomenon, Greenewald began utilizing the Freedom of Information Act (FOIA) to hammer the U.S. government for answers, and he targeted every government agency to get them.

As he waited for answers on this niche of the paranormal, he then branched off to investigate nearly every government secret imaginable. He was a sophomore in high school when he first started his trek in 1996, and he archived all of his research on a website that became known around the world as The Black Vault. Today, he has amassed well more than two million pages of declassified records.

His efforts throughout decades of research have been responsible for getting hundreds of thousands of pages that have never seen the light of day into the public domain. He has appeared on numerous television and radio programs throughout the world and is frequently sourced in various news articles and stories for his archive and his discoveries.